THE ADVENTURES OF AN ACCOUNTANT

An Autobiography

THE ADVENTURES OF AN ACCOUNTANT

An Autobiography

CLARENCE D. HEIN

Mill City Press
Minneapolis, MN

Mill City Press, Inc.
212 3rd Avenue North, Suite 290
Minneapolis, MN 55401
612.455.2294
www.millcitypublishing.com

ISBN - 978-1-934937-69-3
ISBN - 1-934937-69-x
LCCN - 2009922277

Cover Design and Typeset by Sophie Chi

Printed in the United States of America

DEDICATION

To Jane, who let me pursue my dreams.
To my children, who stayed close to me through the adventures.
To all of the loyal, hardworking people at
HEIN & ASSOCIATES LLP (H&A) who helped create
my success story.

TABLE OF CONTENTS

FOREWORD

When I was informed that Clarence was writing an autobiography and that he was going to title the work "The Adventures of an Accountant," I must admit I was somewhat skeptical. What possible adventures does an accountant have? This book answers that question in a unique and simple style, tracing his life growing up in a small town in Montana through an incredible journey that has taken him all over the world. As a lifelong friend, I knew of some of Clarence's experiences and accomplishments, but I was amazed at how much I didn't know of his earlier life and career. This book serves as a testament to what a person can do when intellect, integrity, work ethic and a can-do attitude are molded by life experiences, resulting in significant accomplishments that few people achieve. As I read through the book, it was clear that it would provide his family with a valuable sense of history. It also traces the formation and growth of H&A, which is only one of the legacies Clarence has left to all of us. Family, friends, and business associates will most certainly enjoy and benefit from this book. However, anyone can benefit from learning how one man's journey has resulted in such a full life.

It has been five years since Clarence retired. H&A continues to be successful, his partners and friends continue to enjoy his sage advice, and we enjoy hearing of his travels as he and his wife Jane continue their adventures.

Larry Unruh, Managing Partner,
HEIN & ASSOCIATES LLP

ACKNOWLEDGEMENTS

This book could not have been written without the dedicated efforts of Jill Kannenberg-Doom and my loving wife, Jane. Jill transcribed the book, proofread the results, and ultimately edited the final version. Jane took many pictures over the years, helped me choose those included in the book, and scanned the photos for reproduction. Most importantly, they provided the encouragement I needed to complete the project.

PREFACE

My family asked me to write this book about my life. Actually, it's pretty difficult to talk about myself because the book is really about all of the people that I have lived and worked with over the years. If I talk about myself too much, it is to tell the story of my life from my perspective. I do not intend to be boastful because I know my story was made possible by others.

H&A wants this book as part of their history and has supported this effort. A lot of this book is about my history prior to H&A, but H&A is the biggest part of this story. As you will see in this book, certain events occur in people's lives, and many people do things to propel change in one's life. This certainly happened to me over the years. This story is about my saga of moving from being a farmer in eastern Montana to Touche Ross & Co., a Big 8 accounting firm, to starting H&A. The biggest event of my life story was my marriage to my beautiful wife, Jane, in 1959. This created a partnership that has continued until the present day. Jane was equally as comfortable planning to make curtains for our future farm home as she was entertaining the business leaders in Denver, Colorado or Houston, Texas. Without her support and many talents, my travels through life would undoubtedly have been much different.

My greatest satisfaction in all my years of business and forty-two years in public accounting was all of the people that I was able to help and develop. I am convinced that public accounting is one of the greatest avenues in America for people to learn and develop their characters and business skills.

INTRODUCTION

My parents, Oscar Hein and Rose Strasheim, were born in 1914 and 1915 in Wyoming and Colorado, respectively, to immigrant parents—Ludwig and Christina Hein, and Conrad and Katherina Strasheim. I know very little about the history of my mother's parents. However, my cousin Judy Remmick has spent twenty or thirty years researching our heritage from my father's side of the family.

My dad was the sixth of fifteen children born to Ludwig and Christina Hein. He was born in a homesteader's shack near Torrington, Wyoming, six or seven weeks premature. According to family lore, they put him in a shoebox on the cook stove to keep him warm and prayed. It worked.

Ludwig and Christina Hein were born in Borodino, Bessarabia, a German settlement on the Black Sea, to Michael and Christina (Stohr) Hein and Karl and Katarina (Henke) Schweikert, respectively. They received their international passports, somewhat unusual, as a result of family ancestry to the Harlus family in France. A friend of Michael Hein owned a shipping company in Bremen, Germany, and booked them on the Main for passage to the U.S. This family was also involved in trying to rescue Nicholas II, Czar of Russia, and his family from their execution in 1918.

Michael Hein, my great grandfather, became a respected businessman and the second-wealthiest man in Borodino. He owned vineyards, produced wine, and owned very expensive stallions. Ludwig related to family members the day that

Nicholas II rode into the Hein estate to purchase horses. Col. Daniel Hein, Michael's brother, rode at the head of the Russian Calvary next to Nicholas II.

Michael Hein's father, my great-great-grandfather, was George Hein, who related to Ludwig his memory of leaving Moscow in wagons at the age of five or six to escape the attack by Napoleon. George did not recall being in the wagon as much as he remembered walking most of the way to Borodino.

My great-great-great-grandfather was Col. Mikoel Hein, who was born in Gratz near Warsaw, Poland and moved to Saint Petersburg in 1807–1808. He married Elizabeth Zappolya, the daughter of Julia Radziwill and Prince Zappolya. They were descendants of the kings of Poland and Hungary.

Although the family tree goes back to Frederick the Great, I cannot find proof of certain aspects of that heritage. However, the history through Mikoel Hein is recounted by actual word of mouth from family members.

My mother's parents were born in Frank, Russia, and came to America in 1906. The village of Frank was populated by German immigrants from the Hessen area of Germany at the invitation of Catherine the Great in the 1760s. In the late 1800s, the Germans began to flee Frank because the Czar put an end to all privileges and was determined to make them full-fledged Russians. Many came to the United States.

CHAPTER 1

GROWING UP

My grandparents, as well as Jane's paternal grandparents, came to Sidney, Montana, to farm sugar beets. Sidney is 100 miles south of the Canadian border and about five miles west of North Dakota at the intersection of the Yellowstone and Missouri Rivers. The Yellowstone River irrigation project was one of the first projects to allow irrigated farming in the arid areas of the country.

I was born June 4, 1939, in Sidney. We lived in a tiny house with no running water, plumbing or telephone. Water was carried in by bucket, and there was a wood-burning cook stove. I remember walking to the outhouse when I was three or four years old on cold winter nights—not a pleasant experience. My father worked the family farm with my grandfather, and since tractors were not available, they still used horses.

When I was sixteen years old, I had a very fascinating story of an early memory. I was standing on the streets in Sidney, Montana and saw the chief of police drive by with a very pretty blond girl about my age sitting in the front seat with him. I was sure that I recognized her but had no idea who she was. I told my mother about this when I got home, and told her I was sure that I knew this girl. I said that I remembered seeing her walking in Sidney with her mother. The mother had a dog harness, or some other device, on her to ensure that she did not run away. I also remembered playing with her on our living room floor. My mother told me that this seemed impossible since that little girl's father, the police chief, and her mother, had divorced when we were eighteen months old and she had never been back to town.

World War II was in full swing until I was six years old. Everything was rationed, and it was a major event whenever nylon stockings arrived in town. All the ladies would dash to the stores to get what they could. Apparently, nylon was scarce because it was used to make parachutes. Farm trucks were not manufactured from 1939 through the end of World War II. My dad ordered a new truck around 1943, and I still remember going to pick it up in 1946.

As I mentioned, farming was still accomplished with horses during my early years. My recollection is that we got our first tractor with steel wheels in the early 1940s. Growing up I never got to have a horse. They were hated because once the farmers got rid of them they were no longer going to be welcome on most of the farms, even for pleasure.

A major event occurred in my life in 1943 at the age of four. My dad was chosen to rent and farm the Holly Sugar factory farm. We moved to a big three-story house, with running water, plumbing, electricity, and a five-party telephone line. This was quite a step up in lifestyle and a good opportunity for my dad. The factory farm had a rather large lake that provided water for processing sugar beets. Since we rented the farm, I had unlimited access to the lake to fish as much as I wanted. I put my set lines in the water while the ice was still breaking in the spring, and I didn't even take them out in the fall. I let them freeze when the ice came. When I reached the ripe old age of nine my dad got tired of me bugging him to take me hunting, so he handed me a 16 gauge sawed-off shotgun and told me to go by myself. My first year of hunting was the best. I shot nine pheasants and one duck with twelve shells. I fished at the factory lake into high school, but when I turned ten I also was allowed to go fishing in the Yellowstone River. I rode my bike there, which was two or three miles away, and fished for catfish.

My mother told me that even at an early age I liked to put on a suit and dress up. I never remembered feeling that way, but she had pictures to prove it. The first bad experience with farming—and there were a number of others to follow, as I will discuss later—occurred on a Sunday morning as I was standing in the barn talking to my dad, all dressed up for Sunday School, while he was milking the cow. Unfortunately for me, the cow had to sneeze. The sneeze caused an explosion of cow dung that created a silhouette on the wall where I was standing. Sometimes I think this was an omen of things to come in my future endeavors to be a farmer.

When I was six we took a car trip to California to visit my grandparents, who had left the sugar beet country and moved to the grape country in California. My Uncle John was invited to accompany us on the trip. He got tired of my constant talking during the trip and offered me a dollar if I could be quiet for one minute. Unbelievably, I never earned that dollar.

When I was nine or ten years old, I talked my dad into letting me drive our farm tractor home from the repair shop where he had had some work done. I tried to turn into our driveway from the main road at a high speed, as my bigger cousins often did. Unfortunately, I was not strong enough to straighten out the wheel, and the tractor went around the corner and ran head-on into a cottonwood tree. There was a lot of damage done and our farm work was delayed. My dad complained to my mother that he could not believe how stupid I was not to slow down when I turned the corner. Her response, which I still remember, was that he was pretty stupid to let a nine-year-old drive a tractor.

My parents bought two farms around 1950. One was a dry land farm about ten miles from town, and the other one was an irrigated sugar beet farm across the road from the factory farm that we rented for nine or ten years. This was my home until 1959. When I was twelve years old, I was helping my dad combine our wheat crop on our new irrigated farm. My job was to sit in the truck, read books, and then drive the truck to the combine when the grain hopper needed to be unloaded into the truck. One day a bee got in the truck, and I spent a good bit of time chasing it out the window. I did not realize that in pursuing the bee, I had bumped the hoist lever on the truck. When my dad waved to me to bring the truck to the combine, I started it up and took off. While my dad stood near the combine waving his arms, the truck box was lifted by the hoist and dumped almost a full load of grain into the field. As I asked my dad what we should do now, he handed me a shovel with a slight smile and told me to load the grain back onto the truck. If you have ever lifted a shovel full of red wheat, you know this is no easy job for a 12 year old.

In February 1953, when I was thirteen, a terrible disaster occurred that cannot ever be forgotten. My brother Jerry and I were driving home during the lunch break at Sidney High School. Jerry was concentrating on figuring out how much money he needed to save from his job at Safeway to go to the State Basketball Tournament. He was driving down the road at about fifteen miles an hour, quite unusual since he usually clipped along at about forty-five or fifty, deep in thought. When we got to the railroad tracks, which had no signals, I remember looking to my right to see if the train was coming. The next afternoon, I woke up and saw my parents standing nearby. I asked them, "Where am I at?" They said that I was in the hospital. I asked them why I was in the hospital, and they responded that we had hit the goose, the nickname for the milk train that ran between Williston, North Dakota and Sidney, Montana. My response was, "Bullshit—I don't believe it." We had, in fact, hit the goose head-on.

4

My brother lost his right leg in the accident and had no recollection of anything for six weeks. I was pronounced dead at the scene and placed in the burrow ditch next to the road with a blanket over me. A friend of the family came by in his station wagon, and I was loaded into it and transported to the hospital. Once at the hospital, a faint pulse was detected and, needless to say, I survived one scary accident. My parents, after some period of time, asked me if I would like to see the car involved in the wreck. They took me there and it was quite a sight. I had caved in the metal dash of the 1950 Chevrolet with my head and gone headfirst through the windshield. My upper jawbone was fractured in thirteen places, and I was a total mess. This was certainly not the way one would like to start their first year in high school. My brother was a track star at age fifteen and one of the fastest runners in the State of Montana in the 220-yard dash. It was very difficult for our family to realize that Jerry would never be able to realize his potential in track, and that his life was dramatically changed.

My high school years were a lot of fun. One of the things that made my high school years enjoyable was that I was able to work on the farm as the hired man. As a result, I did not have many days, weeks, or months when I did not have anything to do. Because of the train accident, Jerry could no longer work on the farms, so I assumed all of the farm work duties at age thirteen. We did not have a hired man at that point since my dad and I could handle the farm work for both farms.

Besides working on the farm and going to school, activities included hunting, fishing, football, and cars. I had five cars in my high school years, including Chevys, Studebakers, and a 1949 Cadillac. As compensation for working on the farm, I got a brand new 1956 black and white Chevrolet when I was seventeen, all the gas I needed to burn, and a five-dollar-a-week allowance. I had it made. My '56 Chevy was fast. I could beat anyone in drag racing from 0–60, except one Olds J2. I also set some speed records going from Sidney to some other towns in the area—some in excess of 100 mph. In hindsight, another reason high school was so much fun was that I did not have a girlfriend until my senior year.

I became a poor student in high school because I had decided that I would become a farmer and that I did not need a lot of book learning. Many of my cousins went into farming and did not go to high school at all. I thought that if I graduated from high school, I would have done quite well and accomplished more than many of my relatives. I probably had the ability to be a good student, since I scored high on achievement tests and the IQ test administered in my junior year. When I was in the fifth grade, the teacher posted the math lessons for the week on Monday morning. I always finished the week's work in twenty minutes and was able to work on other assignments she gave me to keep me busy.

One of my favorite hobbies in high school was spot-lighting jackrabbits. We could sell jackrabbit carcasses from fifty cents to a dollar, depending on demand in any particular year. We would go out at night and chase jackrabbits with our cars and spotlights and some days we could pick up as many as twenty and earn ten dollars. It was illegal to hunt jackrabbits in North Dakota. Therefore, it made most sense to us to go to North Dakota late at night when everybody was in bed to chase the rabbits.

When I was a junior in high school I had the opportunity to become an entrepreneur and do a little farming of my own. There were about twenty acres of prairie lying unfarmed on our dry-land farm. My dad told me if I would plow the ground and plant barley, I could keep the net profits for my efforts. After all the labor of working up the ground and planting the barley, bad luck set in. Late in the spring, we had very cold weather that ruined my barley crop. So much for the profits from that effort. My dad made the statement that he had never seen barley freeze in before. That was a statement that I would hear again.

During high school I did all of the work on our five-hundred-acre dry-land farm. My dad would come out and plant the grain in the spring and again in the fall to combine the grain. Other than that, I took care of all the rest of the farm work. One morning, when I arrived at the farm to commence work, I discovered that thieves had stolen the battery, broken the gas line, and stolen the gas from my tractor. When I went to town to buy the parts I needed to fix the tractor, I devised a plan to catch the thieves. I loaded two-by-eight planks, large spikes, and a shovel into the pickup and went back to repair the tractor and prepare to catch the thieves. I dug a trench at the entrance to the farm. I pounded the spikes through the two-by-eights and buried them with the spikes sticking out of the ground so that the next time the thieves came in they would puncture their tires and be caught. After the tractor was fixed, I drove out of the farmyard on my way to do my work. Suddenly I realized I had run over the trap! Air and heavy fluid in the tires to increase traction were leaking, so I had no choice but to head into town to get the tires fixed and replace the fluid, which cost about $125. That doesn't sound like that much money now, but it was two weeks' pay for the average worker in those days.

I graduated from high school in 1957 and ranked forty-sixth out of our graduating class of eighty. I went to college in the fall of 1957, but quit after one quarter because I just did not like college. From January, when I returned from college until farming started in the spring, I needed to have a job to support myself. Jobs that one can find in a small town are not very good jobs. I went to work for the local dairy that had two components. One of them was to drive around in a large truck and pick up milk from the dairy farmers. That part wasn't too bad. The other part of the job was delivering milk to residential customers. This was a bad situation. The milk truck used to deliver milk to the customers had no heater and no door on the side exited to take the milk to the front steps. On those mornings when it was forty below zero, it was a tough duty to earn a dollar an hour. When that job ended, I went to work as a feed grinder for a dollar twenty-five an hour. My shift lasted from four o'clock in the afternoon to twelve o'clock at night and entailed grinding and bagging feed grains and alfalfa for the livestock industry. Grinding alfalfa, which is very dusty, with a lot of clothes on because it is so cold, becomes very uncomfortable because the dust gets into your long underwear.

Jerry, Rose, and Clarence Hein, before indoor toilets

Rose Strasheim and Oscar Hein

Clarence all dressed up with Jerry

Clarence's childhood home, 1939-1943

Clarence at Factory Lake fishing hole

Sidney, Montana

Clarence with his 1956 Chevrolet

The Heins' train wreck

CHAPTER 2

MOVING ON – MARRIAGE, FARMING, AND EMCOE

The winter of 1958 became quite interesting while I was back in Sidney living with my parents and waiting around to get involved in the new farming season that would begin in April. Somewhere along the line during that winter, Jane and I started hanging out together and became better friends, even though at the time we both had other romantic interests.

By March 1958, Jane's dad decided that we were becoming too good of friends, and decided to ship me off to Mexico. He hired both a friend of mine and me to take a sheep train to Mexico to watch over twenty carloads of sheep as caretakers. Our job was to make sure the sheep were fed, watered, and appropriately cared for along the way. We each got fifty dollars for expenses and for our time for this weeklong trip. The trip was pretty uneventful except for in Los Angeles, when we were waiting for the train to return back to Montana. A con man picked us up with a very fine story and was leading us to our demise when a stranger stopped us and asked if he could tag along. The con man disappeared, and our friend, who to this day is still unknown to us, told us that this con man had planned on taking us to a place to be sure that we left with no money or other valuables in our possession. It is amazing how con men can come up with information about your life and convince you that they are familiar with your background, and even the town that you live in. We made it safely home, and Jane and I began dating on a more serious note that led to our lifelong relationship.

In the fall of 1958 Jane left for the University of Colorado in Boulder, and I returned to Eastern Montana College of Education (EMCOE) to give college another try. I was not sure that farming and odd jobs were right for me, but I also really did not like college. By December, Jane and I were both very lonesome and the writing was on the wall—we were going to get married. Once again, after the fall quarter, I quit college. I had learned my lesson. I was going back to Sidney, and I was going to become a full-time farmer.

In March 1959, we had a big wedding at the Pella Lutheran Church in Sidney at the ages of eighteen and nineteen. We were related to almost everyone in town, so the wedding was very large and many of the Danes and Germans in the area attended.

Jane and I made an interesting couple. My background was as a farmer, and my life did not include activities in the social world. Jane's background was totally different. Her dad was a true entrepreneur. Her parents designed a very modern showcase home that was completed in 1948. They had the first dishwasher, freezer, and radiant heat with hot water pipes in the floor. Even the governor of Montana came to the open house. Jane's family opened the Lone Tree Inn, a classy supper club, where she remembers working in the kitchen doing dishes and peeling endless shrimp. This was during the time of the first oil boom that hit the little town of Sidney. By the early 1950s, Jane's house was grand central station for everyone—including the people her dad worked with in his livestock business, the oil guys, the ladies' bridge club, teenagers, and sometimes even out-of-town basketball teams. Jane developed many social skills and also learned that nothing is forever. The sheep business collapsed and the oil boom ended. Her dad never slowed down; he continued in various ventures throughout his life. Of all the people I have met in business, he will always be one of my heroes as an entrepreneur.

We began our married life as full-fledged farmers. We leased two different tracts of land and planted sugar beets, alfalfa, and wheat. I farmed together with my dad and helped him with his farms in return for the use of his equipment. My luck at farming was questionable from the very beginning. After sugar beets are planted, they will often come up and begin growing with rainfall. About half the time, the sugar beets need to be irrigated in order to come out of the ground. In my first year of farming, we had to irrigate the sugar beets twice—which is never supposed to happen—to get them to come up because it was so dry, cold, and windy. This irrigation process works; however, the crop is never as good if irrigation is required this early. By June we had an early hail storm. This hail beat up the beets, making the crop even weaker, and reduced the production from my first cutting of hay and wheat crop by 50 percent. Even so, without a heavy investment in equipment and no debt, I was looking forward to making a very nice profit in my first year.

By summer we began planning for the future. We were talking to my dad about buying a farm that he owned about ninety miles away in Terry, Montana so that we could own our own property. A neighbor to that farm was also thinking about selling. My hope was that if I was going to be a farmer, I could start out as a big farmer early on. Jane had already picked out the curtains for our proposed new house and was planning on making them as soon we could buy the farm. However, more trouble lay ahead. The fall of 1959 was to become the worst year for harvesting beets that has ever occurred in eastern Montana.

By September, a cold rain started falling and temperatures

dropped below normal. When it came time to harvest our sugar beets, the fields were muddy, and there was no way to get the tractors and beet harvesters into the fields to harvest the beets. Eventually it got cold enough that the ground would freeze at night. We would go into the fields at midnight after the ground was frozen, so that the tractors would stay above ground, and attempt to mud out the sugar beets. The beet harvesters would get plugged up with mud, and we would have to stop every hundred yards and clean out the mud in order dig up any beets. The beets were so mud-loaded that we would fill up our beet trucks with 8 tons of beets and end up with 1½ tons net after removing the mud and the tear. This is as opposed to a load of beets in a normal year constituting around 6 tons with 5¾ tons net beets. By November when winter had come, in addition to being hailed out, we had 50 percent of our beet crop frozen in the ground forever. This had never occurred before 1959, and it has never occurred since.

Jane and I evaluated our situation and had some tough decisions to make. Ultimately, I decided that the good Lord had sent me enough signals that I was not to be a farmer and that I should at least have backup plans for the future. We decided that I would return to school at EMCOE and study accounting. By getting two years of tax and accounting education, I could do tax returns and bookkeeping in the winters in addition to farming to ensure that we had a fallback position if our bad luck in farming continued. Jane was going to work to help put me though school, and we would return to farming in two years. We moved to Billings, Montana, at Thanksgiving in 1959 and I started school in January. Jane got a nice job at the local hospital as a practical nurse, and we were set to have enough money to get through school for the next two years.

My parents were not too happy that we were moving away from Sidney. Most of my relatives grew up and stayed there. Even so, my dad hauled the furniture that we had to Billings in a farm beet truck. After we were in Billings for awhile, my mother called quite upset. She said, "You did not have to move away. We received two phones calls—both you and Jane could have had good jobs here." The Chamber of Commerce was looking for a secretary and had called about Jane, and Montana Dakota Utilities was looking for a meter-reader and had called about me. She said we could be making $500 a month and living in Sidney. Jane and I, however, were committed to move forward with life.

Life did not go smoothly for us for very long. In February 1960, Jane fainted on the job at the hospital. The good news was that we were expecting our first child. The bad news was that we were not prepared financially to start our family. We had very little choice. We decided that I would go to work part-time and stay in school. Jane, after the baby was born, would attempt to work part-time to help with our finances. I decided that I would have to carefully manage my time if I was going to go to school and work, so I set a goal for myself to try to maximize the value of my education in a minimum amount of time. I decided that I would try to get straight As in accounting, get Bs in other business classes, and accept Cs in all other classes. The resulting B average was going to be good enough for me. I ended up staying at EMCOE until midway through my junior year in March of 1962. I was doing well in accounting, and my professors were encouraging me to stay in school.

Jane worked part-time during most of this time, and I had a number of jobs. We worked so many hours and had so little time that we saved money during this period because there was no time to spend it. My first job was at Gallagher's Tire & Supply Company. This was a local gas station that sold bulk gasoline, tires, and had a dozen or so gas pumps. I was hired as the bookkeeper during my first quarter of accounting education and also to assist in serving customers. I was paid a dollar an hour, and my working hours were from one o'clock in the afternoon to ten at night, seven days a week. I received no benefits or vacations. I carried fifteen hours of class work in the mornings. I was one busy boy. Mr. Gallagher turned out to be a chronic alcoholic. He married the same woman five or six times when he was sober, but always got divorced after long spells of drunkenness. His wife told me that he never got out of bed until he had finished a pint of whiskey and a six-pack. I wouldn't doubt that, since he had trouble staying on his feet all day. His problems became so bad that I basically ran the gas station for him, kept the books, paid the bills, purchased all products, and became the general manager to take care of this guy.

The bookkeeper that preceded me didn't know a thing about bookkeeping,, so he had plugged numbers, guessed at things, and the books were a general mess. I went back and cleaned up all the books and records to the current date. The accounts receivable listing of customers did not agree to the books. I managed to reconcile that down to being only one dollar off, and then went on to other things, realizing that some day I would come back and look for the dollar. Looking for a dollar seems rather silly; however, the accounting instructors always said, "If you're off a dollar, it could be two large numbers offsetting and resulting in a dollar, so you'd better find it." After I got things cleaned up and settled down, I went back and found the dollar. Low and behold, there was a $10,000 bill to a customer that was never sent out, offset by $9,999 of other differences. I asked Mr. Gallagher what to do with the $10,000 bill. He said, "Send it out!" Guess what? It was paid immediately.

Gallagher was unreasonable many times in his drunken state. One winter, after a snowfall, he told me to go out into the street and clear the ice off the main street of Billings, Montana, so people would have an easier time getting into the gas station. After I chopped the ice for awhile, he came out to see how I was doing. I had had enough. I tossed him the shovel and quit. Since I needed the $63 a week to live on, I set off to find other

18

jobs. I worked at Sears & Roebuck clearing cash registers and doing the daily retail reports on Saturday, and in the afternoons I worked at the County Assessor's Office assessing real estate. I also got a job as a bookkeeper at Daniel's Lion's Den, a fine dining restaurant and bar. After Gallagher called me daily for a month, I agreed to go back and take care of his business and bookkeeping. I received a raise up to three dollars an hour and worked evenings when he was not there. I worked at the Lion's Den from five o'clock a.m. to just before eight a.m., and then went to school. I returned later in the day to handle other matters for the business.

Going to school full-time and working sixty hours a week created a lot of time pressures. One example of how I survived occurred during my cost accounting class. We received the cost accounting practice set on a Friday and were given six weeks to complete the practice set. That's all that would occur during class hours. Students would work on the practice set and receive help from the teachers to get it completed. I decided that this was a real opportunity to have more time in my life. I started the practice set after work on Friday night, completed it, and turned it in Monday morning. I did not go to bed or sleep even for one minute during those three days. My cost accounting teacher accepted the project and told me he would see me in six weeks. It is rather amazing what a person can get done if the need is great enough.

After two years of accounting at EMCOE, they awarded an outstanding accountant of the year award. This award consisted of a brand new accountant's handbook that cost about thirty dollars at the bookstore—quite of bit of money in those days. Even though I did not spend much time at school, I did develop a very good friend in my accounting classes. When I received this outstanding accounting award, he thought that he should have received it. We were no longer friends, and hardly spoke after that. To this day, I am amazed at how some men can be so negative about the success of other people. I still see that type of attitude in some men to this day. I have always tried not to feel that way, after this happened to me, but I suppose it is a little bit natural for men to have difficulty accepting the success of others.

In 1961, I realized from my education and jobs that I could be successful in accounting. I was also not particularly committed to getting a college degree, since I really didn't have the background and knowledge to realize how important getting a degree is to one's future. I saw an ad in the paper advertising for a construction accountant for the Yellow Tail Dam Project. The offered salary was much bigger than anything I had ever seen. I decided that maybe it was time to give up college and get a real job. I interviewed for the job and shortly thereafter received a call from the construction company asking to meet with me again. I went to the second interview very hopeful that I might get the job. Fortunately for me as my life has turned out, the recruiter had a much different answer. He told me that I was by far the most qualified candidate that he had interviewed for the job. However, he said he was not going to hire me because he wanted me to stay in school and get my degree. In its own small way, this was a life-changing event for me.

One hot July day in Billings, I managed to make a lousy decision. I don't recall where I found the time, but we went fishing for rainbow trout at Dead Man's Basin, a lake outside of Billings, for a whole day. I spent the day fishing in a tin boat in my swimming suit and with no shoes on. I never believed that an old Montana farmer could get sunstroke, but I had it big-time. I filled the bathtub with steaming hot water, got in, and shook for about an hour until I could warm up. To this day, my feet cannot be exposed to the sun for very long, as they are so sensitive from being burned so badly that day.

In the spring of 1962, the University of Denver (DU) visited EMCOE to recruit students. Even though EMCOE was a four-year college, they could only grant education degrees at that time. A student could get all of the classes needed for a degree in accounting, but had to take enough education classes to get a degree in education. Therefore, DU visited there on an annual basis to recruit students to go to DU to get degrees in accounting. After their presentation, they had dinner with the students that they wanted to recruit and made great promises. They promised part-time jobs, that they would help find a house, and that they would grant scholarships. Jane and I were at a crossroads. However, it was clear to us that we had a future in accounting, and we thought we might as well go for it and move to Denver. I was nervous about quitting my job at Daniel's Lion's Den. The owner, Bill, had repossessed it to collect on the money he had invested in the place to have it built for the previous owner. When I met with Bill, he was rather upset with me for even considering staying in Billings to help him out and not going to DU. He said, "Get out of town and go get your education."

Our move to Denver was something to behold. We decided that much of our furniture was so old and beat up that it was not worth hauling all the way down there. We saw an ad in the paper about a furniture company that would come to your house, give you a bid for your used furniture, and haul it away for free. We called them and they came to our house. After reviewing our furniture they said they did not want it, but that they would haul it away if we paid for the removal fee. We took the rest of our belongings and headed to Denver in our yellow 1955 Chevy (we had moved down from our 1956 to a 1955 by this time) and a small U-Haul trailer. Our '55 Chevy burned a lot of oil. We could go 300 miles on a tank of gas, but we needed to refill oil every 150 miles because it burned a quart every 50 miles. Gas station attendants were always surprised when we pulled into the station and told them, "Fill it up with oil and check the gas!"

Looking back, Jane and I were pretty gutsy. Here we were,

turning down the job at Yellow Tail Dam and moving to Denver with a promise of a job and a scholarship. That was all topped off by the fact that our son, Mitch, was one year old, and Jane was expecting our second child. At the time we could not understand why our parents thought we were crazy.

Jane and Clarence celebrating her eighteenth birthday

Jane's Sidney home

Road to dry-land farm

Clarence at work on his accounting job at Gallagher's

Yellowstone River

Jane and Clarence's home in Billings

Jane and Clarence's wedding, 1959

Jane and Clarence with Mitch, October 1960

CHAPTER 3

ARRIVING IN THE BIG CITY, DU AND TRB&S

We arrived in Denver in March 1962, just before our third anniversary. We spent the night in a motel on North Federal, and I went to DU the next morning to get started. DU had arranged three interviews for me: one with a local accounting firm, and two with Big 8 accounting firms. They had one of the former students from EMCOE meet me and take me to the apartment in West Denver where we would be living. They provided me with financial aid that consisted of half the tuition for one quarter and a loan for half of my tuition for the balance of my education at DU. I was all set, so I went home to prepare for my interviews the next day. We went shopping at Arlen's to get me prepared for this big day. We bought a green suit for seventeen dollars, a clip-on tie for one dollar, and a white shirt. I was set to go.

My interviews went well. The local accounting firm and one of the Big 8 firms offered me a job as a proofreader until I graduated from college. My interview with Touche, Ross, Bailey & Smart (TRB&S) went better. They offered me a job and said that I could work on the regular audit and tax staffs even though I was still a junior in college. They asked me to divide the amount of money I needed to live on by the hours that I could work, and that would determine my hourly salary so that I could get through college as soon as possible. They felt that I should keep my hours down since I was going to school full-time, and that the most important thing was to get through school. We agreed that I would work thirty-two hours a week.

My recruitment was handled by Carl Griffin, the future chairman of TRB&S, and the recruiting process must have gone pretty well. I had caught a case of the flu prior to this interview and I was not feeling too good. They administered the Wonderlic Personnel Test, which is a type of intelligence test, and I had to take two tests. After the first one, Carl came back and told me that they would like me to take the second one. I apologized for doing so poorly and told them that I was not at my best because of the flu. At lunch, Carl asked me what my hobbies were. I told him that my favorite hobby of all time was spot-lighting jackrabbits in North Dakota. Since he was from Detroit, he was a little shocked. A number of years later I heard that I had achieved the highest score on the Wonderlic Test of anyone that had ever taken it when interviewing at TRB&S.

My first day at TRB&S could have started better: I had never heard of the Big 8, and I had no idea how to pronounce Touche. I was quickly straightened out on the correct pronunciation and went to work. That first winter I prepared individual tax returns. I was frustrated in the beginning because I could not get the returns done perfectly without any corrections by the reviewers. After about a week or two, a lady who worked winters reviewing tax returns sensed that I was nervous when confronted with questions about my preparation work. This wonderful lady told me that having minor corrections for tax return preparation work was normal, and that, in fact, I was the best and most accurate preparer in the firm. I felt much better.

One of the returns I worked on was for an individual who was one of the four founders of the largest toy company in the world. He had invested ten thousand dollars as a founder and was worth in excess of $100 million. He had cashed out several million dollars of stock and ended up owing a large tax bill. My tax supervisor at the time decided that he would begin to teach me how to provide good client service, so he invited this wealthy client to a meeting and told me that I should attend to see how he handled it. The tax supervisor told our client the bad news; he owed a lot of money. He also told him not to worry about it because we had contacts at the bank and would be happy to introduce him to a loan officer to help him get a loan to pay his taxes. The client told the tax supervisor, "I don't need banks; they need me." I think I sensed at that time that it was a good idea never to volunteer to help clients unless it was something that would be well received.

The first audit I ever worked on was a chain of finance companies. This was right after I started to work at TRB&S, so I was doing some menial audit-type work. Interestingly enough, the owner of this company was a client of mine during all of my TRB&S days, as well as at H&A, until he died. Shortly before he died, he met with two people for lunch to say goodbye. He met with his attorney and me.

TRB&S changed its name to Touche Ross & Co. somewhere along the line during my career there. From here on I will refer to the firm as TR&Co., which was its name during most of my career at the firm. Many companies in the U.S. at the time were changing their names to a shorter version as the thing to do. Even so, when people asked me what happened to Bailey & Smart, I always told them that they must have screwed up.

TR&Co. lived up to its word, and I was treated as a regular staff member from the time I started. In the summer of 1962, they told that I would be going to Group I school. This is a two-week conference in Michigan for all new recruits of the firm. It was an incredible honor for me to be able to go to this school while I was still in college. Even more exciting, I got to fly on an airplane for the first time. The flight to Michigan was very exciting, and I enjoyed it a lot. By the time we were ready to come home, however, I had decided that flying was dangerous. I was afraid to fly home but finally forced myself to get on the plane. This fear of flying lasted for five years, and I don't think I really got over it until I had flown a million miles. Jane used to drive me to the airport and my face was whiter than my shirt.

Group I was a major event and very educational. I met a lot of people with the firm, and I still know a number of them. This group school in 1963 was part of the beginning of women in public accounting as a career. We had two ladies out of 160 participants at our school. One of these women was the top student in the school. It was hard for me to accept, but I had to rate her above myself. Ten years later, when I was running the Denver office for TR&Co., she asked if she could transfer from Chicago to Denver as a manager. I jumped at the opportunity because she was definitely in the running to be one of the first woman partners in the firm. Unfortunately, she got married and decided to give up her career.

We had no women staff accountants at TR&Co. until 1964. We were short of staff, and we received an application from a woman who wanted to move to Denver from a large firm in New York. After much prodding, we were allowed to hire her over the objections of who was then the partner-in-charge. He finally agreed to bring her on staff, but made the condition that she would not be allowed to travel, as he was worried about women's safety during business travel. Several months later, the time came when she needed to travel on an audit. The partner-in-charge insisted that it was not safe for a woman to travel, and he objected to her going on the audit. After he was advised that she knew how to take care of herself and carried a .38 pistol in her purse, he finally consented to let her make the trip.

After a few months at TR&Co., our first daughter, Melanie, was born. Jane had two babies to care for and I was working pretty much full-time and going to school full-time. I had a class at seven o'clock in the morning and at eight, then went to work at nine and returned to school to take another class at night. But things were good. I made a higher salary and worked fewer hours than I did in Billings. We also made enough money to take care of the babies and buy a few pieces of furniture from time to time on credit. Dick Graham, who had just graduated from dental school, and his wife, Toppy, were our first neighbors in Denver. They had their first baby about the same time that our daughter was born, and our friendship has continued from then until now, some forty-five years later. One Sunday morning, Jane set out to plan a party. Two-year-old Mitch decided to scatter cornflakes all over the house. To be helpful, I hooked up the vacuum cleaner and vacuumed and vacuumed. The more I worked, the more the cornflake dust flew all over the house. The place was a mess! When Jane came home to the disaster, we discovered that I had plugged the hose into the wrong end. This was my first and last housekeeping effort.

My first year at TR&Co. in 1962 went very well, and I had many great experiences. I had one problem on an audit that was difficult to understand, and even today I scratch my head as to why such a thing happened. I was sent out to perform some basic audit work on a large paint manufacturing company late in 1962. In checking the mathematical accuracy of the inventory, it became apparent that there were numerous mistakes and that the inventory accuracy was not acceptable for the audit. I brought this to the attention of my audit supervisor, and we decided to meet with the controller to discuss this issue. The supervisor told the controller that they should reject the math on all the inventory calculations because of the large error rate. The controller told us that he did not have the time or the people to redo the calculations, so that was really not going to be feasible by the time the audit needed to be done. I suggested to the controller that they consider hiring comptroller operators, who could very quickly and at a reasonable cost recalculate all of the inventory figures. The controller took exception to this recommendation and called the head of the TR&Co. office, and had me removed from the audit the next day. This was a tough lesson learned, and I was forever careful about making suggestions and the manner in which they were made for many years. If possible, it is sometimes best to let others come up with their own solutions with a little help getting there.

I received more good career news early in 1963 after about a year with TR&Co. I was going to San Francisco to the Group II audit school. This school is for audit staff members preparing to become seniors on audit engagements. I think the Denver office needed special permission to send me, since I still had more than a quarter to go to graduate from college. Even though I considered not going because I did not want to fly, this was such a big career opportunity I had no choice but to suck it up and get on the plane. I was a little embarrassed at the school one evening because at a group dinner each person had to get up and tell the group which college they attended, when they graduated and what they were doing at TR&Co. at the time. A lot of people, many with masters degrees and two years experience, looked at me strangely when I said that I was going to graduate from DU in June and that I was planning to start assuming senior audit responsibilities on some engagements.

After going to Group II school in March, I seniored my first engagement for a large food processing company in May of 1963. Since I was in school until nine a.m. every morning, I was told to tell the client that I needed to go to the office each day to do certain things so that the client did not know that I was going to school. In July 1963, just after graduating, I seniored an audit of a large potato chip processor.

I took the CPA exam in May of 1963 while still in college. When the results came back in August, I had passed all parts of the exam and became a CPA. Graduation was in May of 1963 and the commencement speaker was the President of India. My parents attended my graduation and I think were a little shocked that one of their kids had actually graduated from college. After performing so poorly during my first two attempts at college, my parents had been reluctant to provide any further financial assistance. However, my dad did loan me half of my tuition to be repaid when I graduated. At my graduation, he forgave that loan of one thousand dollars, which was a very nice graduation gift indeed!

Early in my career, TR&Co. decided that I had enough potential to warrant upgrading some of my personal traits. I still wore white socks to work because white socks are good for your feet when you work on the farm and wear boots and other work shoes all day. My audit manager explained to me that, in the business environment, white socks were in poor taste. Also, early on, the firm decided that attending toastmasters would be good for me to improve my communications skills. Toastmasters was a wonderful experience, and I attended religiously every week for two and a half years. Toastmasters is a two-year program where there are twelve speaking sections to be completed. After two and a half years I had gotten through eleven, and I decided my skills were adequate for me. Even though I never became a great public speaker, I was able to get through some major speeches to business groups, and I even delivered speeches to two national real estate conventions in New York and Miami.

In November 1963, the world experienced another disaster. John F. Kennedy was assassinated in Dallas, Texas. Everyone remembers where they were when the assassination occurred. I was driving from Pueblo, Colorado to Denver, Colorado after having observed an inventory in Pueblo. A couple of days later, we were watching the news regarding this assassination and witnessed the shooting of Lee Harvey Oswald live on TV.

During my early years at TR&Co., I worked on a lot of manufacturing companies. These included the food processing company, the potato chip processing company, a company that had changed from making wagons pulled by horses to making drilling rigs on the back of trucks, and a national paper and envelope manufacturer.

I uncovered a few fraud and embezzlement situations in my early years. I was brought in to prepare bank reconciliations for the bank accounts of a national paper manufacturing company. Even though they were public, they did not have time to reconcile their bank statements for a whole year. In doing the reconciliations I found fraudulent checks, which, after investigation, proved to be a theft of the company's checks from the check printing company. Since this did not involve any internal employees, it was a great relief.

One day I was sent out to count cash and do inventory work at an auto parts store. When I got there, the money for the day's sales was not in the cash drawer. The manager explained that he had taken the money to go buy more parts and that as soon as they arrived he would have invoices to support this position. Needless to say, he was caught.

I also worked on a plumbing company that had large contracts to install the plumbing for homebuilders and others. I discovered that the company recorded all of its sales but never reduced its inventory to record the cost of its sales to expense. The financial statements were grossly overstated and, when corrected, showed that the company was in quite of bit of trouble. When the controller and I advised the bank officer of the problem and told him that we had new financial statements, he said not to bring them down for a month or so since he was going on vacation and did not want to deal with the issue at the time. These experiences were not that huge in the big picture, but they did help prepare me for dealing with more serious financial statement fraud matters later on in my career.

In 1964 life was going along quite smoothly, so it was time to shake it up again. I decided that I wanted to buy an accounting practice and go into business for myself. I researched towns that had too few CPAs for their population. I also ran ads in regional and national magazines. I ended up with two good offers. One was in Boise, Idaho and the other in Grand Junction, Colorado. I decided to buy the practice in Grand Junction, which was being sold by a seventy-five- year-old practitioner who wanted to retire. My reason for deciding that it was a good idea to buy my own practice was that I found auditing rather boring, and I wanted to do something more interesting. The reaction from TR&Co. surprised me quite a bit. It was not unusual for Big 8 firms to hire staff, train them to some degree, and then have them leave. In fact, they have always been known to have somewhat of a revolving door. However, TR&Co. did not react well to my leaving. After a short period of time, they advised me that they were going to do something that they never did. They told me that there were no guarantees but it was highly likely that I would be a partner in the firm. They thought it would be a very unwise move for me to leave that possible opportunity. At that point, the whole national firm of TR&Co. only had about eighty partners, so the likelihood of making partner was quite significant. I apologized to the gentleman in Grand Junction as I withdrew from the deal, and his response was that he was not a bit surprised.

By 1965, my career was in for a major change. I was offered the opportunity to become the report reviewer for the Denver office. In those days, the report reviewer was a partner in each office of TR&Co. who reviewed all audit and other accounting engagements for final approval before issuance; reviewed all engagement letters for audit, tax, and management services; and reviewed any special letters regarding advice to clients. This person was the last line of defense for TR&Co. to ensure that all of its work products were of the highest quality. This position was required to be a partner by TR&Co. The Denver office had received permission to put me in charge of report review even though I was just becoming a supervisor, as long as I met several conditions. One of those was to attend report review training in New York for six weeks. I would have to stay there the entire six weeks as the firm was not willing to incur the expense to fly me back and forth for weekend visits at home with Jane and the kids. The other conditions were that I read all accounting and auditing literature that had ever been produced two times and all Journals of Accountancy for the past ten years. I also was to read four textbooks regarding management skills and business concepts, and all technical letters that had been issued by TR&Co. regarding all technical questions that had gone to the national office since the beginning of that process. I agreed to these conditions, and off I went to New York. I worked in the New York office during the day doing report review and read accounting literature every night and weekends to get this project done. I lived in a hotel near Central Park and worked at the TR&Co. office on Wall Street. I rode the subways to work but sometimes walked from Wall Street back to the hotel—a distance of about ten miles. A number of years later I asked the partners why they had picked me for this project. Their answer was simple; they thought I was the only one who would actually do it.

While in New York I ran into my second con man. I think this time I was better prepared. I was having a beer at the bar of my hotel one evening before dinner. A Native American Indian approached, sat down beside me, and bought me a drink. He had a hat on and talked about the Wild West and seemed somewhat knowledgeable about Sidney, Montana. Eventually he said he was having a party for Gandhi and that he wanted me to come to his apartment with him. Since this story was rather nonsensical, even after a couple of beers, I told him where to go. He told me that I should stay on my stool and not move before he left or he would shoot me. I told him to start shooting because I wasn't going with him.

I took over report review in 1966, and this became the most educational experience of my life. I reviewed every accounting and auditing job and read every tax letter, management services report, and engagement letter for many, many clients over several years. In reviewing reports, everything had to be perfect. This also was the age of multilith machines, and if any errors were discovered, every page had to be retyped. There was no other way to correct mistakes. I saw a case where a report of sixty pages of numbers had a mistake on the last page. It affected every page, and all sixty pages had to be retyped. What a nightmare for the typist and proofreaders. My job included making sure every amount, dollar sign, and word was properly presented before anything went to typing. Amazingly enough, white-out, which would enable corrections to be made without retyping, did not show up for a couple of years.

My career was going well. After getting rid of my white socks, learning to be a better speaker, and taking over one of the most important functions in the Denver office of TR&Co., I was ready for the next stage of my career. Just five short years ago, I had taken off my rubber irrigation boots and started college. I began to wonder at this time how I could have made such a large transition in life and have such a good grasp of business without any background enabling this process to occur.

Clarence and his parents at his DU graduation in 1963

Jane and Clarence with Mitch and Melanie in Sidney, 1962

Clarence gets his turkey!

Mitch and Melanie with Great Grandfather, Johnston,
who drove stagecoaches over Trail Ridge Road in Colorado

CHAPTER 4

CLIMBING THE LADDER AT TR&CO. TO PIC

I graduated from the University of Denver in 1963, made partner in 1969, and became partner-in-charge (PIC) of the Denver office in 1971, just after my thirty-second birthday. This has always seemed like a fairy tale to me, because it generally took five years to make supervisor, seven to eight years to make manager, and ten to twelve years to make partner. It seemed that from the time I entered public accounting, I could always understand what made a business tick and what management should do to be successful. Genes play an important part in our lives, and somewhere along the line I picked up some genes related to accounting and the business world. Having grown up on the farm in eastern Montana, I had never been anywhere outside of the state except for two automobile trips to visit grandparents in California when I was six and nine years old and the sheep train experience when I was eighteen years old. I was now in the right place at the right time, working for an accounting firm that was willing to let me progress and learn as fast as possible.

After living in our first apartment in Denver and in two different rental houses, an opportunity to buy our first home came along in 1964. A co-worker at TR&Co. had a friend and neighbor who was in desperate need to sell his house as a result of a divorce. The house was in Westminster, Colorado, in an area where the market was probably close to thirteen thousand dollars, and the seller was willing to take eleven thousand. However, the house and yard were a mess and had not been cared for. The grass was dead, the front door was hanging by a hinge, and the house had not been painted since it was built and had the old-style speckled paint in each of the rooms. I made a deal with the seller to give him a down payment of one hundred fifty dollars, a second mortgage for one hundred fifty, and assume the GI mortgage with an interest rate of 4.25 percent. Our house payment was one hundred and four dollars, and our second mortgage payment was two dollars.

Very pleased with the deal that I had made, I went home to tell Jane that we were buying a new house and that we should go look at it. Some wives get very excited when they purchase their first home and have tears of joy. Much to my chagrin, Jane's reaction was not very good. She immediately looked at the house, began crying, and said, "I do not want to live here." After about a half hour of discussing plans to fix up the house and rejuvenate the yard, we agreed that, even though this was not our dream home, we would fix it up and become homeowners, and that after we developed some home equity we would move on to bigger and better things. We were able to realize enough equity from the Westminster home to move to a nice ranch home in Wheat Ridge four and half years later in 1968.

The years from 1963 through 1971 were fast-paced, as I was in charge of the report review department and responsible for quality control for the entire Denver office. Since these were internal responsibilities, I was also available to perform many special projects for the firm. This was the beginning of a career during which I did numerous special projects of all types throughout a period of forty-two years. Some of these projects that I worked on have remained in my memory for many years.

One project that I worked on was for a children's hospital in the mid-60s. The controller had installed one of the first mini-computer systems and after two years could not get the books balanced in order for the hospital to get their financial statements. The controller was reluctant to ask TR&Co. for help and things were not getting any better. When the controller went on vacation for two weeks, the hospital asked me to straighten out their books. After hiring a data processing center to reprocess all of the transactions of the hospital for two years, I printed a trial balance and began the audit. When the controller came back two weeks later, needless to say he was rather surprised.

It came as quite a shock to me when I was assigned to due diligence projects for proposed business acquisitions. Some of our larger clients were acquiring other large companies, and in the mid-60s I was sent out to St. Louis to perform a due diligence review for the acquisition of a large company. Since these types of transactions need to remain secret, I went to the company disguised as an IBM salesman so that I would be able to talk to anyone in the company about financial matters on the basis that I needed information to evaluate possibly upgrading their computer systems. The project went quite well. Both the buyer and the seller were very happy with my report. The seller, however, was disappointed in the fact that I discovered something negative, and they asked me to leave it out of the report. When asked whether or not I was willing to remove the comment, I stated that I did not think it was appropriate. The comment stayed.

I was young when I took over the report review department and was naturally a little bit concerned about the support I would receive in the event that a disagreement would arise between a client and the position that TR&Co. or I would take. Art Samelson, who was a founder of the office and the PIC when I went to work there, brought me into his office. Everyone was a little bit afraid of Art since he definitely had an aggressive personality. Art sat me in a chair in front of him and began his little talk with me. He explained to me for several minutes that my job was to protect him, the office, and the firm. He told me that if I ever backed down from him, a client, or anyone else at TR&Co., I would be fired. Art never wavered from that commitment and stood steadfastly by me through a number of difficult client issues over the years. From my observations of the situation in other offices with other report reviewers who were partners, I believed I was in the strongest position in all of TR&Co.

In another engagement in the mid-60s, a company came to TR&Co. seeking assistance to evaluate the acquisition of a competitor. I was assigned the project of helping the client evaluate the acquisition and advising them during the transaction. Shortly after being engaged, the client approached me and asked me to negotiate the entire transaction for them. After a thorough evaluation of the deal, I concluded that the seller was in so much financial difficulty that a fair offer should be made, but that offer should be quite a bit less than the asking price. I told our client that if the seller did not take our offer, the seller would probably end up in bankruptcy court. The client could then buy the assets at an even cheaper price than our offer. During our meeting with the seller, they rejected the offer. Subsequently, however, our client was able to buy the major assets of the seller from the bankruptcy courts.

I was assigned to do my first litigation support case in the mid-60s. My client was one of the largest steel companies in the U.S., which provided steel pipe for the laying of a pipeline to bring water to the Denver area. The contractor claimed that the pipe was not always perfectly round, and therefore they suffered damages because they could not weld the various pieces of pipe together without incurring additional costs. Eventually, I sat through the entire trial with the attorneys at the front desk advising them each step of the way and testifying for the first time in front of a jury. The case had a successful outcome. As my career unfolded, I worked on many litigation projects as an expert witness and was also heavily involved in defending TR&Co. and H&A in various matters.

Also during the mid-60s, I took over responsibility for the public company clients that were subject to the Securities and Exchange Commission (SEC) reporting requirements. My involvement in SEC-reporting companies continued throughout my career until I retired.

One of the more shocking and intriguing experiences that I had during this timeframe was in 1966 while I was still a supervisor at TR&Co. The executive vice president of one of TR&Co.'s largest and wealthiest client families from New York City came to Denver to repossess an office building on which they had made a second mortgage. I was assigned the project of working with this executive to analyze the financial status of the building, help with the repossession, and close on the transaction. Several days later, just after the closing, we were walking down the street in Denver, Colorado. This gentleman told me that I should go into Art Samelson's office and demand that he make me a partner. I told this client that that was pretty much out of the question, since I was only a supervisor and had only been with the firm for four years. He said that I should do it, since he had already told Art that he should make me a partner, and that he had worked with many other partners at TR&Co. and I was more competent than many of them and ready to be a partner. I obviously never took that path; however, it may be one of those events contributing to my early promotion to partner a few years later.

Another shocking event happened during the same timeframe around 1967. I had worked on a small audit for a client who had real estate properties in South Dakota. After finishing my work and reviewing the financial statements of the companies with my client, I learned that he was somewhat concerned about the liabilities of the companies and their future cash flows to meet their obligations. I didn't have much to do on the plane ride back to Denver, so I started doing cash flow forecasts for these companies and completed them when I returned to Denver. These cash flow forecasts showed clearly that his companies would be fine and had adequate cash flow to survive and service their debt. After I sent these to the client, he called and was obviously very relieved and thankful for the work that I had done. Even though the work was not part of the engagement that I would be paid for, it seemed like the logical thing to do, as the client needed it. Also, the companies were small enough so that it did not take a great deal of my time to do this favor for him.

A number of months later, I was sitting in my office and received a call from this client. He asked me to come to South Dakota and meet with him at nine o'clock the next day for fifteen or twenty minutes because he had something very important to discuss with me. He said that he could not give me any more information, but that I could rely on his judgment that it would be a worthwhile trip for me to get on the plane and be there for the meeting. I flew late into the night to get to a connecting airport and then took an early morning flight into the small town in South Dakota. The client spent about fifteen minutes explaining a project for which I had just been hired. The client and a wealthy industrialist from another state were taking over the management of all of the funds of the royalty family of a Middle Eastern country who were unhappy with their New York money managers. They would be managing all of the funds for all 150 members of the royal family, who controlled most of the assets of the country. He handed me two acquisition agreements and told me to be prepared to work on these acquisitions as they were closing. He also told me to arrange a tax deferral system for the multimillions of dollars that they were going to receive at the front end of this project to take on the work. Not only was this potential client staggering in scope, I was also concerned about the reaction of some of my associates in Denver because they were Jewish and we would be taking on this Middle Eastern family as probably our largest client. When I got back to the office, I explained the project to our top tax professional, who was Jewish and who would be handling most of the heavy lifting for the tax work. He said, "No problem. Go tell Art." He did not think there would be any concern, and there wasn't. In fact, their reaction was that if this client relationship came through, I would probably be the youngest retired partner in the history of the firm.

As is obvious from the fact that I worked for another thirty-seven years, things did not go as well for me as they could have. After we had done quite a bit of work for tax planning, the Middle Eastern family decided not to bring their investments to the United States, but instead switched them to the United Kingdom as the United States financial markets were entering into some troubling times. This would be the first of a number of troubling times in the financial markets that would affect my career throughout the years.

In 1964, I uncovered fraud during an audit of an industrial bank in Aurora, Colorado. Of all the fraud situations that I have seen in my career, this one was discovered in quite a unique way. In auditing finance companies and industrial banks, one of the audit procedures is to confirm loans, deposits, and certificates of deposits. It generally takes at least two mailings of confirmations and much effort to get 50 percent of the confirmations to be returned by the customers. In this particular bank audit I noticed, when working late in the evenings, that the president was always in his office typing. It seemed strange to me that the owner and president of the bank would be working at night and doing his own typing and not having it done during the day by his clerical staff. Also, the certificates of deposits confirmations came back with outstanding results. Not only did the returns exceed the 50 percent that I was hoping for—confirmations for 90 percent of the certificates of deposits came back. After I finished the audit, I reported my suspicions to the audit partner in the Denver office. I told him that the confirmation results were far too good and that this late-night typing seemed strange. It was a little tough to approach the owner and president of the bank and accuse him of fraud based upon these facts. However, the audit partner sat the audit in the corner of his office and did not do anything to issue the report. We waited it out. After three or four months, lo and behold, the newspaper reported the discovery of a major fraud at an industrial bank in Aurora, Colorado.

In 1968, the biggest event of my career occurred that helped propel me towards early partnership and future management positions within TR&Co. The national headquarters of a large TR&Co. client had moved to Denver. The company was on the New York Stock Exchange, owned bus and trucking companies, and was acquiring other businesses. The audit partner had me perform an extensive report review of the audit and financial statements. My review lasted several days, and I was able to come up with good suggestions for the audit team and the company. Later in the year, the audit partner transferred to the east coast as PIC of a large office. Since he had been the only audit partner in Denver, the Denver office partners approached this client and suggested that a senior partner in the office, who was a tax person and administrative partner, become responsible for the company's accounting services. I think much to everybody's amazement, the client said, "We don't need a partner...put Clarence in charge of our audit." This put somewhat of a strain on TR&Co. because I was a new manager and had only been out of school for about five years. To top it off, the company decided to do a public offering of some bonds on Wall Street shortly thereafter. Obviously, I was put to the test in a big hurry. I had never done a registration statement for an SEC company, so I read all of the manuals and books available to get up to speed. The offering went quite well, and I was surprised to learn during the meetings in New York with the underwriter, the underwriter's counsel, and the company's counsel that no one seemed to know much more about an offering than I did. I felt somewhat comforted because the former partner for this company, who was in his mid-50s and from Chicago, came to the meeting to help me through the process. The offering went effective and the Chicago partner and I headed for home.

On the flight from New York to Chicago, the Chicago partner asked me how many SEC registrations I had been involved with. When I told him none, he was not surprised, and his answer was "me neither." I came to find out that nobody in the room at the final closing of the offering had ever worked on an SEC registration, including the New York attorneys and the representatives of the underwriter, except for the underwriter's counsel. After this series of events I was never intimidated working on any engagement, no matter how difficult the project. I realized at a young age that I could probably know as much about most subject matters as others involved, if not more, if I put forth the effort of getting up to speed with adequate research and preparation. Even though a partner was required to sign all financial statements issued by TR&Co., I signed the registration statement with the authority of the firm as a manager at the ripe old age of twenty-nine.

In 1968, another event occurred that provided for many fun family vacations for many years. Jane's dad called and told me that he had made a deal to buy a ranch on Rock Creek in western Montana for one hundred thousand dollars. The 160-acre ranch included a house, a sixteen-unit guest lodge, and extensive lake frontage. Rock Creek also ran through the property. The seller was a wealthy individual who had developed the first hotels with swim-up bars. He had run into difficulty with a relationship between his younger wife and his son, and he was disgusted and ready to leave town and unload the property. Jane and I decided to help Jane's dad with the down payment since he was low on cash, and I went to the bank to get the money. The PIC of the Denver office took me to the First National Bank of Denver and explained to them that I wanted a loan to buy an interest in this ranch. The banker asked me whether I was really sure I wanted to invest in a Montana ranch having never seen it. I told him that I was going to treat my investment as a gift and not count on ever getting it back, since that is often the case in business transactions with relatives. The banker gave me the loan. This turned out to be a good decision because I eventually got my money back with a good return, and our family enjoyed vacations at the ranch for many years that included great fishing, horseback riding, and camping in the mountains.

In late 1968 or early 1969, I was made manager-in-charge of the entire audit practice for the Denver office. Since we had no other audit partners, I had total responsibility for hiring, firing, training, client service, and quality control of an entire audit practice. I established some unique management styles during this phase of my career that continued for many years. I developed a very open and honest relationship with everyone working under me, provided them with financial information regarding the performance of the department, and made sure they knew where their performance stood in relation to their coworkers by using a performance rating system.

In 1969 I was promoted to the partnership of TR&Co. I enjoyed managing the audit practice. It was a challenge to handle the New York Stock Exchange client and other companies, and I continued to do special projects such as mergers and acquisitions. I also liked to visit the subsidiaries of my client companies, as I always felt better signing off on the financial statements if I knew the people and business operations that existed around the country. This turned out to be popular with some clients. Eventually some of them would invite me to spend a day or two at their facility to talk about their business. They rarely asked me questions, so I wondered why they wanted me around. I eventually decided that they just liked to talk to me about their businesses and read my reaction to determine whether or not I thought they were on the right track.

The CEO of our New York Stock Exchange client was generally known throughout the country as the toughest New York Stock Exchange CEO. His employees described to me his theories of being an effective leader. His theory was that leaders have to be liked and respected. Liked did not mean going to social events together or hanging out together, but meant that people enjoyed working for the executive. Respect did not mean that he was the greatest at anything in particular; it meant that people were a little fearful of him as a strong leader but also knew that he would be fair. I found over the years that these criteria are quite accurate.

In 1969, one of my clients who had a rather volatile personality tried to hire me, which was about his fifth attempt to get me to go to work for him. One day while driving through the rain, he asked me what it would take for me to go to work for him, since he was ready to do whatever it would take. I told him that it would take one million dollars a year. This was a lot of money in 1969. His response was, "Am I really that bad?" We continued our great relationship in the future up until the date that he passed away.

In 1970, our family was blessed with the birth of our son, Michael. Mick, as he is known, was a problem birth and took five complete blood transfusions. When he was born on an emergency basis, our family doctor stuck a tube in his throat and breathed for Mick until they could get the blood types back to start the transfusions. Before the fifth transfusion, the doctors told Jane that he may not make it because he was too weak for another transfusion. Jane told them to get their butts down there and do the transfusion. She said, "He will be just

49

fine." Well, Mick did turn out fine, and our gamble to have a third child knowing that we had a blood incompatibility issue came out fine in the end. This blood incompatibility known as the Rh factor often causes stillborn births. The shots that solve Rh problems for people now did not exist when we had our first child in 1960.

Dennis, Jerry, Clarence, Rodney, Oscar, and Rose Hein, 1966

CHAPTER 5

THE PIC YEARS AT TR&CO.

The PIC of the Denver office of TR&Co. suffered a serious stroke in May 1971 in Honolulu, Hawaii. Because of his incapacitation, three of the older partners of the Denver office were appointed to jointly manage the office until a future course of action could be determined. As time went by, it became clear that a new PIC would be named for the Denver office. Even though I had just turned thirty-two in June of 1971, it appeared to me that I was just as qualified as anyone else in the office to become the new PIC. However, because of my age, I also assumed that there was a strong possibility that a partner would be transferred to Denver from another office for this position.

In September or October of 1971, the chairman of the board of TR&Co. came to Denver to interview candidates to become the new PIC. He interviewed two older partners and me for the position. The new PIC of Denver was going to be one of the three of us. Nobody was going to be moved to Denver. The chairman of TR&Co. who was conducting the interviews was the same person that interviewed me when I was first hired by TR&Co. I am sure he remembered that my favorite hobby was spot-lighting jackrabbits. One of the toughest questions during the interview was what I would do in the event that I did not get the PIC position. My answer to that question was that I would do everything I could to support the person who was selected as the PIC, but that I would expect to go onto another career position in the future.

In November 1971, I received a telegram from the managing partner of TR&Co. in New York. The telegram advised me that I had been named the PIC of the Denver office, and that I should tell the other partners in the office that I had been appointed to this position. I was a little surprised that there was not more fanfare in obtaining such an important new job, but I called a partners' meeting of the other partners to advise them of the telegram that I had received. The meeting was very short. I told the partners that I had received a telegram and that I was the new PIC of the Denver office. I told them that I did not know what they were going to do, but I was going to go home and drink martinis. That was the end of the meeting.

The day after being named PIC, I held a meeting with all personnel in the Denver office to let them know what was going on and answer their questions. The key focus of the meeting for me was to communicate my philosophy to everyone present. I told them that I had concluded that, even though I was very young, I could be successful in my new position if everybody helped me, and that without their help, I would fail.

Obviously when this promotion occurred I had more than a full-time job doing other things, including running the audit department. I decided to delegate everything, except those responsibilities appropriate for the PIC, to other people immediately. I also moved to a new office, leaving behind everything that I did not want to be responsible for in the future. Whenever matters came to me in my new office that did not seem appropriate for the PIC to handle, I sent them back down the hall for somebody else to deal with. I also gave my administrative assistant and executive secretary authority over all administrative matters and personnel. I believe these two decisions early on in my new position enabled me to step up to my new responsibilities and develop a very smooth running organization in a short period of time.

Within days of my promotion, it was time for Jane and I to change our lifestyle to appropriately reflect the image of the PIC of TR&Co. in Denver. We bought a new home in the Cherry Ridge area of Cherry Hills Village in southeast Denver and applied for membership to Cherry Hills Country Club. Jane was sent to Neustetter's, the nicest women's apparel store in town, to purchase a new wardrobe. She was treated very well and even had one of the Neustetters involved to help supervise her makeover. Her one-day shopping spree cost us about ten thousand dollars in 1971. I was sent to Homer Reed Ltd. for my new wardrobe to be supervised by none other than Homer Reed, the owner of this high-end men's store. On top of all this, we bought new furniture and our china, crystal, and silver were all updated to provide enough complete place settings to entertain appropriately in the future.

Part of being a partner and PIC of TR&Co. is a need for a personal banker. The personal financial commitments to undertake this new position were significant. In addition, I soon found out that being a partner in a Big 8 accounting firm required significant contributions to capital, which are often based on income. I spent several years educating my banker as to the reasons why each year when I received a raise, I also needed additional bank borrowing. I needed to invest ten thousand dollars more in capital for every ten-thousand-dollar increase in salary. Also, the ten-thousand-dollar pay increase required a payment of five thousand in income taxes. Therefore, every time I received a raise of ten thousand dollars, I needed to borrow an additional five thousand to pay my capital contribution and income taxes. The banker that I used during these early years never forgot this strange financial arrangement. He and I have stayed in touch for over thirty years, and we still laugh about the difficulty I had explaining my need for a new loan every time I got a raise.

In February 1972, I received some good news and bad news. TR&Co. had been given the opportunity by the American Institute of Certified Public Accountants (AICPA) to provide a chairman for a new real estate committee to draft new accounting rules for the real estate industry. The real estate industry was in a hot streak, and many deals were being made without adequate rules to govern the accounting for profits on the sale of real estate. The Securities and Exchange Committee (SEC) was very upset with the situation and demanded that the AICPA develop new accounting rules for real estate or they would do it themselves. In those days, the AICPA was very sensitive to these matters since it was critical to maintain accounting rule-setting in the private sector as opposed to allowing the government to take over. I was asked to chair this committee because I had expressed interest in real estate accounting. The executive office from New York listened to my concerns about being a new PIC, having major client responsibilities, and just being pretty busy learning how to be a PIC. I received no sympathy. They gave me forty-eight hours to call them back and inform them that I would take on this project. Since I had no choice, I accepted.

Another wrinkle was added to this project when, at the first meeting, I found out that the new real estate accounting guidelines would need to be approved by the Accounting Principles Board (APB) before it was replaced by the Financial Accounting Standards Board (FASB) in August of 1973. So, from February 1972 until August 1973, our committee set to work in an attempt to complete this project in eighteen months. The new rules would have to be approved by both the APB and the SEC by that time. This was a huge undertaking, as the normal time to complete an accounting position paper of this magnitude for the AICPA was 10 to 12 years. We got the project done.

This was one of the most interesting projects that I was ever involved with during my career. The chief accountant of the SEC and his staff called me near its completion and threatened to kill the whole deal unless a disputed paragraph was changed. I managed to convince the committee to make the change in the interest of saving the project, even though the issue involved had been hotly contested within the committee. Towards the end of the project, many letters were received and taken into consideration and public hearings were held to obtain industry comments. Even though not many real estate companies showed up at the public hearings, we received several telegrams from them threatening to file lawsuits to stop publication of these accounting rules. In August 1973, I attended the last meeting of the APB to get their approval for the new real estate rules. On September 1st, the FASB would replace the APB as the accounting rulemaking body, so if the APB did not approve the rules, they would not get on the FASB agenda for several years, and the result would be that the SEC would publish their own accounting rules for the real estate industry. The chairman of the APB was very upset that the new accounting rules were being pushed through so quickly and that the APB was being forced to approve them without a chance to make revisions. I was even called a few names that cannot be repeated in good taste. These accounting rules for the real estate industry were approved by the APB and later, with very minor modifications, adopted by the FASB. They still exist today in 2008, so our eighteen-month project has stood the test of time for thirty-five years.

As a result of this involvement with the real estate committee, I was given another monumental project regarding the real estate industry in January 1974. TR&Co. had received an SEC sanction prohibiting them from taking any new real estate clients, among other matters, until they had published a complete real estate accounting and auditing manual to be approved by the SEC. I began this project in early 1974, completed the 1,400-page manual by May, and received approval from the SEC in August 1974. I was advised on short notice that I needed to be in Washington at nine o'clock a.m. in several days for the meeting with the SEC for the final approval. Since I had an important meeting in Albuquerque the day before the SEC meeting, time was tight. I flew to Albuquerque for the meeting, then to Los Angeles, where I caught a red-eye to Washington arriving at eight a.m. I shaved and changed suits and shirts on the plane and made the SEC meeting at nine. The SEC only had one comment on my 1,400-page manual. They objected to my sample footnote indicating a ten-year amortization period for start-up costs. I agreed to take out the ten years and put in a blank instead of ten. The manual was approved! This project took an incredible effort. I worked from nine in the morning until midnight, seven days a week, from February through May of 1974. I worked on the manual every other week in Denver and New York City. When in Denver I took care of Denver office business from nine to eleven in the morning, then moved to the Brown Palace Hotel, where I rented a room to work for the balance of the day. The real estate manual was published by Commerce Clearing House.

After being named PIC, I visited the former PIC on a weekly basis. He could no longer come to the office because of his physical impairments from the stroke. One of the things he told me was to be sure that Jane and I went on vacations alone. He said that clients would always show up whenever he went on vacation. Even when he would try to get away from everyone, someone would find out, and his vacations always ended up including clients. He emphatically believed that his stroke was partially caused by the fact that he never really got away from work and totally relaxed. I have always taken this to heart throughout my entire career, and Jane and I have been to many remote vacation destinations.

In 1972 or 1973, TR&Co. conducted a review of its retirement program in order to make modifications to make it financially viable in the future. The retirement benefits were too rich and needed to be revised. In conducting this review, the chairman of TR&Co. visited Denver. During his visit he shared some information with me that was rather shocking. Even though I had been the PIC of Denver for a couple of years, I was still the youngest partner out of three or four hundred partners in the entire firm. Under the partnership agreement as it existed, my retirement benefit at age sixty-five, assuming normal inflation, would be one million dollars per year. Two things were clear to me from this discussion: all of the partners in the firm were going to retire before me, and the plan certainly needed to be changed.

As PIC, I delegated responsibility and authority to my partners. I provided a lot of information regarding performance of the office, departments, and partners; set measurable goals; and made sure that everyone could see their performance relative to everyone else. Given the freedom I allowed my partners to make decisions and succeed, everyone had a ladder to be as successful as they wanted as compared to their peers. One of the motivations became the fear of failure. Motivated people like to be first in terms of their performance measurements, not last. Whenever I have mentioned the fear-of-failure concept as being something that motivates people, I receive criticism that this is a negative thought process and not positive. However, an organization functions with great motivation and a positive attitude when its leaders have the authority and information to succeed, whether one would call this competitive process a ladder to success or creating a fear of failure.

A year or so after becoming PIC, I received a great compliment from one of TR&Co.'s large and successful clients while walking down 17th Street in the financial district of Denver. This client met me on the street and said that he didn't know what I was doing, but TR&Co. had become the best Big

8 firm in town. He said that TR&Co. partners provided great client service and stood prepared to make decisions on behalf of their clients. He also told me that none of the partners of the other Big 8 firms were willing to make a decision on their own, and that they always needed to go back to their office or national office for decisions. I was very excited by his comments and have always encouraged partners and staff to make decisions on behalf of their clients that are appropriate under the circumstances.

I learned another very interesting lesson during these early years of my career. I called the CEO of our largest client in Denver and asked him if he would introduce me to the CEO and Chairman of the Board of the largest bank holding company in Denver. Although I was nervous to make this request, my fears were quickly resolved. Our client told me that he would be happy to do it and that people in his position do very much enjoy helping other people get ahead in their careers. My meeting with the bank Chairman and CEO went very well, and he again assured me that it was exciting for people in positions like his to help others with their careers.

This reminded me of an experience that Jane and I had early in our marriage, while I was attending college in Billings. Jane was working part-time for the Caterpillar dealer and heard that they were looking for somebody to sweep their front parking lot. She told her employers that I was willing do this type of work since we needed the money. I spent most of a Saturday sweeping the driveway and received twenty-five dollars. Although this wasn't a lot of money, it was actually better than the one dollar an hour I had received from other employers. Shortly thereafter, the owner of the Caterpillar dealership invited Jane and I to lunch at their home in the nice part of Billings. He and his wife told Jane and I that they were very excited that we were working towards our future and getting an education. They told us that their most exciting times in life were when they were struggling

THE ADVENTURES OF AN ACCOUNTANT

to make ends meet, and that those early years were really more satisfying than their later years when they had it made.

Soon after I became the PIC in Denver, the accounting profession went through one of its major changes. Since the beginning of the accounting profession, CPAs were not allowed to solicit other firms' clients, advertise, or quote fees for new business. All of these requirements were intended to keep the accounting profession at a high level of professionalism; however, the world changed in 1972. All of a sudden, CPAs could bid on accounting work and the rules regarding solicitation and advertising were relaxed. Since I was not one of the good ol' boys, I embraced these new rule changes a little quicker than some of the other accounting firms. We started pursuing business in areas of interest, including hospitals and banking. In almost two years, we added a number of hospitals and fifty or sixty banks to our client base. My interest and excitement in growing and developing accounting services would last throughout my career.

During this time, TR&Co. began providing consulting services to banks on a national basis to develop paperless or electronic banking. The largest bank holding company in Denver was interested in this new concept and hired TR&Co. to provide consulting services. I was invited to go with the consultants to a number of the bank meetings to provide a local contact for TR&Co. I remember thinking that the entire process sounded impossible to achieve and pretty far-out. However, many of the concepts that were put forth are currently part of the paperless environment.

One of the most difficult situations that I became involved in soon after becoming PIC was dealing with a partner who had been transferred to the Denver office to head up the management consulting department. This individual was an extremely poor manager in my estimation. His people didn't like him, which is always a bad situation, and they had cause for the dislike. This partner even dug through people's wastebaskets at night and read discarded trash of his staff. I wondered why he had been transferred to Denver; however, since he had married the secretary of one of the national directors, I had the sinking feeling that he was sent to Denver because he needed a job and wasn't particularly successful. I flew to Chicago to meet with the managing partner of TR&Co. and tell him my concerns. He told me to immediately dismiss this department head and to replace him with a consulting manager in the department who was quite competent. I terminated the department head that night and called the manager that I wanted to promote to run the department to have breakfast the next morning. At the breakfast, the manager was very appreciative of my offer to make him a department head, but he advised me that he had just accepted a job as the head of the IT department of a major Denver company. To top it all off, the national director of management consulting for TR&Co. was unhappy with me and told me that he would never help me replace the department head or support the department in the future. But then I got a lucky break. The manager who had decided to go to the large Denver company was unhappy there and called to ask if he could come back. I told him the job was still open. He returned, and between us we were able to make the department successful without national support.

At the age of thirty-three, I became involved with assessing potential litigation issues that TR&Co. encountered against the firm for client services. After being involved in a couple of these, I decided that it was not something I really liked to do. I was sent to Dallas to review a client situation that created a litigation threat against TR&Co. My final analysis was that the office and the national staff had made mistakes in accepting this client. My written report, which went back to the national office, was fairly critical of their process and procedures. I assumed that the national office would not appreciate my negative comments and that I probably would not be assigned any more of these projects. Fortunately or unfortunately, the national office called back and told me that they liked my report and were extremely impressed that I spoke the truth. Therefore, they said that more of these projects would be assigned to me in the future. During this same timeframe, when I was thirty-three years old, I was assigned as the senior national litigation partner on a major lawsuit involving a large company on the west coast. When I asked what a senior litigation partner did, I was told that I would make all of the decisions on behalf of the firm while working with the litigation counsel for the matter. To this day, I'm still astounded at the level of responsibility that TR&Co. was willing to assign to me at such an early time in my career.

In the early 70s, I was named to the National Accounting and Auditing Committee of TR&Co. This committee assisted the national office in reviewing and setting major accounting and auditing positions that would be taken by the firm in serving its clients. In 1975, TR&Co. decided it would change the rules for recording income for the health club industry. Because I served on this committee, I received a lot of input from the industry and was able to affect the outcome of the new rules that were adopted.

Also in the early 70s, the Nixon administration imposed price controls. We had a full-time CPA/lawyer assisting us in advising our clients, as these controls were difficult to enforce. We tried to audit one tanker-load of heating oil from the refinery to the final point of sale. After auditing forty-seven different sales and transfers for this one load, we decided it was impossible to resolve. Even though heating oil left the refinery at a controlled price of nine dollars a barrel and was sold to various cities for up to thirty-six dollars a barrel, even future litigation could not prove the proper price-control ceiling.

My job was not all work and no play. Jane and I went to a partners' meeting in the Bahamas, and I attended a PIC annual meeting in Bermuda. These would be our first trips offshore, but there would be many more to come. Interestingly enough, our international travel occurred with H&A and not with TR&Co. On our trip to the Bahamas, we stopped off in Miami, Florida, where I gave a speech at the national convention of retail land sales companies. I did not impress all of the attendees at the meeting, since they were very unhappy with the new accounting rules being imposed upon them. After receiving a nice applause, one of the attendees raised his hand during the question-and-answer period and told me that he thought accountants should be digging ditches and not messing up their businesses. After our stop in Miami, Jane and I went to New York and spent a day or two on our way to the Bahamas. This was Jane's first trip to New York, although I had been there a few times before on various business matters. In fact, Jane had never been east of the Mississippi River before.

In 1973 or 1974, I became involved in another matter involving employee fraud within one of our clients. The president and his son were changing almost all of the documents related to product purchases in order to keep their vendors happy. The controller approached the audit staff and offered to give them some clues as to where fraud was occurring, but insisted that we not disclose that he advised the auditors of the situation because he would lose his job. After investigating the fraud and documenting the situation, we met with the company's board of directors and legal counsel. The results of the situation were quite interesting. The controller was fired because the company assumed that he must have been the one that disclosed the fraud. Management, however, was not terminated, which is unusual in these situations, and of course, TR&Co. was fired as the auditors. I eventually testified before a judge for the Department of Agriculture, and TR&Co. did not receive any adverse consequences in the matter.

In the fall of 1974, I received a shocking phone call. TR&Co.

was looking to transfer a partner to Houston, Texas, to become PIC of the Houston, San Antonio, Corpus Christi, and Austin offices. Our family discussed this possible transfer at length. We were not very familiar with Houston, so I did some research by looking at the world almanac and other information. The opportunity looked very promising because of the dynamic business climate in Texas. We did have one major hurdle to overcome in making the decision: Melanie had just bought brand new red skis for the upcoming ski season. Our kids were great skiers, and the purchase of new skis or boots was always an exciting event. However, in the interest of a tremendous career opportunity, we all agreed to go to Houston.

I attended an annual meeting of the PICs of the TR&Co. offices after I had accepted the move to Houston. One night, as I was returning to my room and walking with a senior partner of TR&Co. and one of its original partners, the senior partner relayed some rather incredible information to me. He said that the Board of Directors of TR&Co. had been discussing partners who could potentially become managing partner of the entire firm in the future. He said that I was on a list of five partners that they had selected and that my move to Houston would provide valuable experience to me for my future at TR&Co.

Jane catches a barracuda at Kona, Hawaii in 1968

Melanie, Mitch, and Mick in 1974

Our Cherry Hills home in 1971

Moose Lake Ranch in 1977

Family picture at Moose Lake in 1977

CHAPTER 6

THE YEARS IN TEXAS

In October 1974, I started commuting to Houston to take over my duties as PIC of that office and the other three sub-offices. The first big event that I attended was to a large office party for business associates, friends, and alumni of TR&Co. at Houston Country Club. There were probably three hundred people at this gala, and I wore a sports coat, tie, and slacks. Little did I know that Houston is a very formal town, and businessmen always wore black suits for business occasions. My attire turned out to be a big plus, because everybody thought from the very beginning that a new person was in town who was willing to make changes. My feeling was that a change was overdue in the management of the Houston office. I met a TR&Co. alumni at the party who managed the administrative functions for a large Houston law firm. He became a good business friend who introduced me to a number of opportunities over the years. One person he introduced me to was a realtor who handled a lot of the high-end business in Houston. We bought our first house through this realtor, and he proved to be a good friend who introduced us to Houston society very effectively.

I had spent three years as PIC in the Denver office and would now spend close to three years as PIC of the Houston offices.

We frequently entertained clients, business associates, and office personnel during our three years in Denver, and Houston would continue this tradition at an even faster pace. It seems as if we were out on the town at least five nights a week, and by the time I decided to leave TR&Co. in May of 1977, we had become very entrenched in Texas. It was very hard to leave the many friends that we had made and the business opportunities that Houston presented. It was necessary, however, to move back to Denver to start my own business. It was also very difficult to sell our beautiful home, but selling our boat was the most difficult. In fact, when the buyer of our boat showed up to pick it up, Jane tearfully stayed in the house and could not watch as he hooked it up and drove away.

House-shopping in Houston was quite interesting, as the semi-retired senior partner of the office insisted that he be allowed to look at any house that we considered buying. (He believed that it was critical that we own a home that would be appropriate for the PIC of Houston.) We finally chose a home in west Houston in the Tanglewood area north of Woodway. This house met with his approval and was extremely nice. The home was totally remodeled, had 5,200 square feet and six bedrooms, and was previously owned by a man who had moved to Washington D.C. to take over the Washington Post. We moved into our new home in Houston on December 7, 1974. I remembered this date because we had moved into our house in Cherry Hills on December 7, 1971, when I became PIC of the Denver office. Jane again showed her style and class by deciding to have a neighborhood party one week after we arrived in Houston. Our new furniture for the house had not even been purchased and half or more of our boxes of belongings from Denver sat around the house unpacked. I think everybody in the neighborhood came to our party, and we were quite surprised that most of the neighbors did not know each other even though they had lived there for a long time. I think that Jane's insistence that we throw this type of party spontaneously demonstrated our ability to move to a new city and make an impact immediately.

When I took over the Houston office, I immediately became the Senior Partner for three of the largest clients of TR&Co. in the whole country. As Senior Partner, I was responsible for all client services for these companies, and in particular, for all major accounting auditing and decisions for these New York Stock Exchange companies. It still seems strange to me that I held the title Senior Partner at the ripe old age of thirty-five. Some time after I had moved to Houston, I found out that one of the major reasons for my being made PIC there was to handle all accounting decisions for one of the largest clients of TR&Co. That company was a difficult audit client, and TR&Co. had previously required that the former PIC of Houston and two out-of-town senior partners make all the accounting decisions. In effect, the decisions were made by committee and needed approval of two out of three people. The company insisted that TR&Co. name a partner in Houston that could make all of the decisions relative to their account. I was comfortable with this responsibility and felt totally confident to seek help from others when needed.

After moving into our new home on December 7, I went to the office for my first day at work as a resident of Houston. Prior to that I had lived at the Hyatt Regency for four to six weeks when I was in town. December 8th began a long and difficult time for me. The manager of one of our oil and gas clients came into my office and told me that he had discovered financial accounting fraud at one of our clients listed on the American Stock Exchange. Because of limited resources, there was no one but me to handle this crisis. The manager and I undertook the investigation and resolution of the financial reporting problems and ultimately reissued the financial statements six months later. During that time, I worked in a war room from noon until three in the morning seven days a week. The semi-retired partner I previously mentioned always came to work at five in the morning so that he could go play golf by noon. He was quite surprised to notice that every morning, when he signed in at five a.m., I had been the last person signing out in the book at three or four in the morning. During the mornings I worked in the office doing my normal PIC functions and preparing to reorganize most of the office operations. My schedule was so busy working these hours seven days a week that I even did recruiting late at night. When I interviewed Bill Sikora to take over our tax department, I scheduled the recruiting dinner at midnight on a Saturday night. On Sunday morning, I drove Bill to the airport to catch his flight home and returned to the office to work.

Events occurred during my first week in the office that enlightened me to the work I needed to do to get the office operating in a manner that would be satisfactory to me. The Senior Audit Partner walked into my office a few days after I started and told me that he was disappointed that he did not get the PIC job. He told me that he would do whatever I asked, but that I should not expect anything more. He also told me that I had a reputation of expecting my partners and employees to take responsibility for their actions without being supervised on a day-to-day basis. He wanted me to know that he was only going to do what he was asked and that I shouldn't be surprised when it didn't work according to my expectations. I told this partner that he was correct in that I expected people to take care of their responsibilities without supervision, and that one of us would not be around in six months if he continued to maintain that attitude. The bookkeeper also came in about this same time and wanted me to know that she really did not like working there, and she wanted me to know that in case it bothered me. We mutually agreed that I should get a new bookkeeper and that she should move on to a new job opportunity.

I discovered that the office had high turnover in its administrative personnel. There were approximately thirty administrative staff, and the office hired twenty-five to thirty new staff each year and paid employment fees. The secretaries all reported to different partners, and even the typing pool reported to the PIC.

It was a time for a change in that area. I went to a headhunting firm and asked them to find me a new office manager to take total control of all administrative functions for the office. They sent me a number of candidates who were mostly male. None of these candidates met my criteria, so finally the individual who was helping me at the employment agency told me that their office manager was not very happy there because the lady managing the agency and her did not get along very well. I hired their office manager, Leona Laughman, as my office administrator and gave her total authority over all administrative functions and personnel in the office. The one guideline that I did give her was that I did not believe in secretaries per se and that administrative assistants should assist the partners as opposed to secretaries. All personnel would report to her and not to partners in the future. The head of our typing department cried on my shoulder over this change in policy, and my administrative assistant did the same. However, they both ended up staying and being great contributors to the office for many years. Many other personnel had to leave, as they were not willing to accept the changes, having inappropriate relationships within the office, or just not up to the standards set by Leona. I developed many of my concepts on how to manage an office from a book, *Up the Organization*, written by Mr. Robert Townsend, who reorganized Avis Rent-A-Car. In his book he described the merits of using typing pools, as opposed to secretaries, and having executives place their own phone calls as opposed to having secretaries place calls for them. I followed many of the procedures outlined in his book in managing accounting offices throughout my career.

The personal secretary to the former PIC came to me about

a month after I started at the office and told me that she was going to quit, since she wanted me to have complete freedom in hiring someone new. I told her that she was doing a great job and that she did not need to leave. She said that she was still going to leave because she felt that was the best thing to do. She was also about a year from receiving retirement benefits, so I called the national office and arranged for her to stay on the personnel records long enough to receive retirement benefits. This was a bit of a shock to her since the office had a history of creating ill feelings with people leaving the firm…those leaving were not treated particularly well or fairly.

I decided to recruit a new administrative assistant within the office if I could find one. The secretary to the management consulting department met my criteria, and I offered her a job. It took her awhile to decide to accept because I placed a requirement on the job that was not totally to her liking. I told her that if she was going to work closely with the PIC, which she had to do in this new job, she could not date anyone in the office. Ultimately, she accepted the position and became a great help to me during my time in Houston. I made some immediate changes in the way things were done with respect to my job. My administrative assistant opened all of the mail, routed the mail to those involved, and brought the completed projects and responses to me after the work was completed in the event that I needed to review or sign anything. Matters not requiring my attention were handled completely by my assistant and others within the office. Also, each month a large box of financial information arrived from the national accounting office. Immediately I designed summary reports to be filled out for me so that I only saw in a summary form those matters that effected my management of the office. Unless I requested specific reports for detailed analysis, the details in the boxes were gone.

The reorganizing of the offices began immediately. Weekly meetings were held early in the mornings for all partners to set new goals, objectives and operating policies. Within six months, all partners had new responsibilities. Also, TR&Co. transferred two partners and an audit manager to the Houston office and I hired Bill Sikora as head of the Tax Department. The audit manager, Lou Marinos, is a good friend today since I approved a moving budget that included his future wife and her two kids, and a miscellaneous item for one thousand dollars with a picture of a boat next to it. The partners had never seen the office financial statements and were never held responsible to meet their profit plans. All that changed overnight. Not only did the partners get to review the financial information and plans, I held monthly meetings with all partners, managers and supervisors so that they all clearly understood our financial results. I transferred the head of the management consulting department in Houston to run the Austin office because the biggest market there was consulting services. Formerly the office had limited its practice to tax and auditing, which was a very competitive market, as everybody preferred to stay and work there after graduating from college. Also, the competition in Austin was with big consulting offices that offered discounted audit and tax work to help pay the overhead costs. I named a manager in the Corpus Christi office as the manager-in-charge because he had grown up there and had many local connections. Even though it was a small market town, he tripled the volume and ultimately became a partner in TR&Co.

Our tax department also needed to be reorganized in order to function in a manner acceptable to me. The department did a lot of low-level work and utilized talented people with master's degrees to prepare simple tax returns. None of the large audit clients used our tax department for any kind of tax advice or tax preparation. It took almost a year, but we eventually got rid of the low-level tax work and began doing high-level tax work for all of our major audit clients.

One of the biggest challenges that I faced in Houston was

creating a new marketing program in order for the office to grow in accordance with expectations appropriate for the marketplace. The office had a marketing plan that entailed voluminous reports of detailed information that were totally ineffective. We eliminated the entire system and established a new one that was geared towards niches. We organized people within specific industries and had monthly meetings to discuss goals and accomplishments. I asked everyone from supervisors on up to get involved in marketing, and many of them told me that they did not like marketing nor did they have the time. I eventually got everybody involved by asking only for what I could get. One manager who said he didn't have the time was surprised when I gave him the goal of having lunch with a client twice a month. He thought that was easy and joined the bandwagon. The bottom line of this approach was that people who were not initially interested in marketing and sales found that it was fun, and they got involved without a whole lot of prodding. So very quickly we had almost everybody in the office involved in marketing. I named this approach to marketing "organized chaos," a term marketing personnel never accepted.

The final change that needed to be made to be effective in growing the office was to change the policies of the office. I found when I got there that the office was only interested in getting new, large listed companies. They had no interest in getting smaller companies that needed help in growing. This was a root cause of the office not acquiring any new clients for a period of years. Studies show that most companies engage their auditors at an early stage of their life and that they are not likely to change them very often in the future. By eliminating small companies as potential clients, there was little chance of getting enough new business to grow the office. We got this philosophy changed and even started servicing our smaller clients more effectively.

Another impediment to growing and obtaining new clients

was that the former employees (alumni) were a very disgruntled group. A high percentage of new clients for Big 8 firms came from happy alumni working for companies. TR&Co. had a lot of unhappy alumni. I had the office help me identify the alumni who were the most unhappy with TR&Co. and who were bad-mouthing the firm around town. I personally called all of them and invited them to lunch. At the lunches, I never asked for these alumni to refer business to us. I did ask them to agree to quit bad-mouthing the firm and to give me a chance to succeed. They listened to my personal appeal, and most of them agreed to give me that chance.

The summer of 1975 was very trying for Jane and I. I think the Good Lord puts us through periods in our lives to test our strength. Soon after we arrived in Houston, we discovered that we were expecting our fourth child. With all of the efforts required to make the move to Houston and undertake our new responsibilities, this pregnancy was of great concern because of our Rh factor history that tends to worsen with each new birth. It was even difficult to find a doctor who was willing to deliver Michelle. The goal was to deliver her as soon as possible because of the Rh factor. The blood tests showed that Michelle's lungs were developed and that the Rh was a problem in late June of 1975. A second set of blood tests confirmed these findings, and Michelle was delivered on an emergency basis on June 30, 1975. Much to everybody's horror, Michelle's lungs were not developed and the Rh factor was not an issue. After many challenging days at Texas Children's Hospital, Michelle, as we all know, survived. Two days after Michelle's birth, however, my Dad passed away of complications from minor surgery in Montana. I told Michelle to pull off the miracle and get better, and headed to Montana for the funeral. This was easily the toughest week of my life.

The 70s were difficult times for American businesses. In the mid-70s, the entire real estate market collapsed. I think just about every real estate company and developer either went into bankruptcy or went through voluntary reorganization, if the banks were comfortable with existing management. During the same timeframe, political payoffs to foreign governments came to the forefront. Companies such as Exxon and Tenneco were found guilty of having made bribes to foreign officials in the hundreds of millions. Even the aircraft manufacturers got in trouble. Even though the Department of Commerce had held seminars to teach them how to obtain foreign business, they were attacked for making illegal payments. As a result, the Foreign Corrupt Practices Act was passed that required all audits to have procedures in place to look for illegal payments to foreign officials. TR&Co. escaped any consequences because of payments by our clients; however, I did have to deal with certain issues regarding financial reporting of certain transactions discovered by our clients.

The Texas business environment was a lot different than my experience in Denver. The Texas business community operates more on the "good ol' boy" theory. In Denver, if a company requested audit proposals, it was normally four or five firms submitting proposals and fighting for the work. In Houston, I would often receive a call from a company asking to discuss their audit with me. I would go to the meeting with the owner of the company, and he would tell me that TR&Co. was recommended by a friend and that he wanted us to do the audit. If he liked us, he would often say, "Give me a price and get started in the morning." Also, the numbers in Houston were larger than I experienced with Denver companies. One morning I received three calls within an hour from audit partners regarding issues involving write-offs for reserves for losses totaling $500 million for three different companies. This was quite a change from my experience in Denver, where our largest clients had revenues of $200 million.

In another case we were selected as auditors by management

of a company. When management took our engagement letter to the board of directors for approval, one of the directors was upset with TR&Co. because we had charged him too much for his tax return. We lost a significant audit. This director was one of three brothers who had inherited an interest in the largest oil discovery in the history of the United States. Their father had invested in the discovery well when the driller approached their house on a rainy night and asked for $500. Their dad took $500 out of a coffee can and invested it in the well. Nothing was in writing. That $500 resulted in a 25 percent interest in the largest oil field ever discovered. So I put my hat in my hand and walked through the underground tunnels in Houston to meet with one of the other brothers. I told him the circumstances regarding their tax work and that TR&Co. had made a bad decision and that we wanted them all back. This gentleman not only gave us the work back, he also became a friend and sponsor for future new business. The world probably has a lot bigger "good ol' boy" network than any of us are really aware of during our careers. However, one must realize it exists and be sure to operate their businesses appropriately.

Our time in Houston was not all work and no play. As is common in Texas, I flew on private airplanes for hunting trips and to the Super Bowl, and was able to enjoy fishing in the great Texas outdoors.

We bought a lake house on Lake Livingston, approximately 100 miles from our home. The house was on the water and became a regular weekend place for our family to enjoy boating and fishing. All of us became good water skiers. Despite many of the good aspects of the house, it also had major flaws that were very frustrating to me. When I bought the house, I was very careful to be sure that it had an attached garage to store our boat. After we closed on the house, we headed for the lake with our boat to enjoy our first weekend. We stopped at a country store along the way to pick up some beer. The lady at the store told me, "Buddy, this is a dry county—we don't sell beer here." We arrived at our new lake house, disappointed that we had bought our weekend playpen in a dry county. After arriving at the house, we backed the boat into the garage to discover another big disappointment. The boat was one or two feet longer than the garage and didn't fit. I just couldn't believe that I'd bought a lake house in a dry county with a garage that was not big enough to hold my boat.

Our son Mitch also enjoyed the great Texas outdoors. He and a friend roped and caught a ninety-year-old snapping turtle on Lake Livingston. After the turtle dug a number of holes in our backyard, we donated it to the Houston Zoo, where it became the oldest and largest turtle in the exhibit. Mitch also surprised us one Sunday morning as he came limping downstairs from his upstairs bedroom. We immediately asked him what happened. We then found out that, at age fifteen, he and his friends had been going to a small town outside of Houston and competing in bull riding contests. The prize money was good and the organizers of the rodeos were allowing kids to ride based on their own free will.

Melanie also enjoyed Texas and made many friends. On her first date, at age fourteen or fifteen, her date arrived in a pickup with a camper shell on the back. Our neighbors were in shock that she was out with a guy in a "motel on wheels."

In late 1976, the Houston office received a chance to obtain a new NYSE client. The referral came to me from a TR&Co. alumni that I had met two years before, at the first big party where I attended in my sports coat. Jane and I had maintained contact and had become friends with this gentleman and his family. We invited them to go water skiing with us at the Black Bass Marina, where we went boating prior to buying the lake house. The Black Bass is rather rustic, and this gentleman sat down on our couch in the Black Bass mobile home where we were staying only to have the leg of the couch go through the floor. Luckily it did not make any difference, since he eventually referred the NYSE prospect to TR&Co. Working on this audit proposal was quite a coup for the Houston office. They had never been through anything like it. The proposal request came a few days before Christmas, and we had to present it to the board a couple of days after Christmas. Everyone in the office got involved in working on the proposal—the typing department typed it on Christmas Day, and our partners and partners from other TR&Co. offices visited all the subsidiaries. Our proposal was presented on December 28th or 29th and we were successful. Arthur Andersen, who had the dominant office in Houston and was as large as most of the other Big 8 firms put together, was very upset that they had lost this proposal. They grumbled that they had never lost to TR&Co. before. The overall work and teamwork by the office for this proposal was quite an achievement.

A couple of months after we obtained this new NYSE client, the national office gave me a goal to acquire two more NYSE clients in 1977. I inquired of them as to how many NYSE clients the firm had in its goals for the entire country. When they told me that the total firm goal in the country was four and that Houston was to get two, I was quite shocked. I think Houston only had thirty or forty NYSE companies out of seventeen hundred in the U.S., and yet I was given the goal to acquire 50 percent of new NYSE clients for the firm. When I inquired as to their reasoning, they told me that they thought they would give me a goal of two since I had proven that I could do it. At this time, the client that we had obtained in Houston was the only NYSE client TR&Co. had obtained that year.

While in Houston, I traveled every week during the entire time that we were there. Besides traveling to each of the sub-offices once a month, there were numerous other trips related to client activities. One of those trips sticks in my memory quite clearly. On Thanksgiving Day, our family was enjoying the holiday at a condominium we had rented at Aransas Pass on the Gulf of Mexico. I received a call while I was there telling me that I needed to go to the Houston airport and leave for a meeting in New York the next morning. They told me that my secretary already had my plane tickets and would meet me at my house to help me get organized to leave. The next day I attended a client meeting at a large investment banker on Wall Street. Our client had invested $200 million in a company that had just received a qualified opinion subject to going concern from its separate auditors. That put my client's investment at jeopardy. I was asked to fly to San Antonio, Texas to attend a board meeting to get assurance that our client would support this investment so that we would not need to qualify our opinion. I agreed to make the trip; however, I advised our client that Jane and I had 160 people coming to a Christmas party the night of the board meeting, and it would be impossible for me to get to San Antonio and back home in time for the party. It just wasn't feasible for me to skip my own Christmas party, as 160 Houston business leaders were coming to my house. The client agreed to fly me home on a corporate plane after the board meeting so I could attend my party. So off to San Antonio I went, attended the board meeting, and arrived home just in time for the party. Interestingly enough, six months or so later the circumstances regarding this client's subsidiary deteriorated and I made another trip to New York to deal with the consequences of this subsequent event and its effect on our auditor's report.

After two years in Houston, I felt like my goal of reorganizing the office and getting everything back on track was done. My long workdays were over, and I was able enjoy life and do just about anything I wanted to both professionally and on a personal level. In April 1977, I was on a trip to New York and coincidentally got on the plane with Bill Sikora in Houston. Bill had done an incredibly good job in reviving and managing the Houston office tax department. In addition, we had become good personal friends. We sat together on the plane, and after a few martinis started talking about the possibility of leaving TR&Co. someday and starting a new accounting firm. This was unusual for me because I was such a loyal, hard-working, and committed partner of TR&Co. As the days went by, I spent more time evaluating either staying with a large company or being a partner in my own accounting firm. Ultimately the positives of being my own boss won out, and I decided to retire from TR&Co. at the age of thirty-seven. On the one hand, it was a good time to leave TR&Co. Office earnings were up 300 percent from the time I had arrived in Houston, the office had obtained eighteen new audit clients in the last nine months, including the only NYSE client in the firm, and I had achieved great satisfaction in my accomplishments there. On the other hand, it would also be very hard to leave. Our family had developed many great relationships and friends in Houston and had become attached to the southern lifestyle. On top of all that, a large manufacturer of personal computers had contacted me to serve as an advisor to their board of directors to assist them with managing the fast growth of the company. My contact on the board was concerned that most fast-growing technology companies grew so fast that they ultimately failed. On the day before my scheduled meeting with the board of directors, I called to cancel the meeting and told them that I would be leaving the Houston area to return to Denver.

After I resigned, I thought that I was treated in an unusual manner in terms of my relationship with TR&Co. I realized later, however, that it wasn't particularly unusual as this type of treatment is common among large companies. After I submitted my resignation, TR&Co. ignored me for several months. When I called them to remind them that it was probably a good idea to begin selecting my replacement since I would be leaving in three weeks, I received threatening letters from them regarding my future business activities. Subsequently, a day or two before my final day with the firm, they called to offer me a 40 percent pay raise and guaranteed that my income, as well as the other partners in Houston, would be treated in accordance with compensation appropriate for a top-rated office. This type of approach used by large companies in these matters still doesn't make much sense to me. The idea that you ignore, threaten, and then attempt to retain seems backwards to me.

As I was leaving TR&Co., I had breakfast with the head of a headhunting firm based in New York to get his advice as to opportunities that could be available to someone with my experience, in the event that I decided not to go back into public accounting. His advice to me was that I was leaving the best job that existed, and that if I wasn't happy with that, I probably should go buy a McDonald's. I also received an invitation to lunch by a senior partner at a large law firm. He told me that he would be willing to arrange the money for me in the event that I decided that I would like to buy a company in the Houston area.

Finally the truck arrived to move our things back to Denver, Colorado. The partner that told me he wanted the PIC job when I first got there had changed his attitude from wanting the job to wanting me to stay. He sat on our fireplace all afternoon as the truck was loaded, hoping that it was all a dream and that the truck would go away. While the truck was being loaded, I received a call from the executive vice-president of our largest client. He told me that they had had a meeting at the company, and that he had been directed to call me to ask me to change my mind and stay in Houston. I felt a lot of sadness in leaving Houston, which had been so good to us for three years. On the other hand, it was time for me to go on to my own destiny. I wanted to be my own boss and see what I could achieve on my own.

Jane and Clarence at a Houston party at our home
for TR&Co. friends and clients

Our Houston home, 1974-1977

Jane and Clarence at Black Bass Marina and Motel

Clarence—the PIC of TR&Co. Houston

Our boat on Lake Livingston

Mitch's turtle in the backyard

CHAPTER 7

THE BEGINNING OF H & A

Before writing about the history of H&A, it is exciting to review its achievements through 2007. H&A is a $50 million accounting firm, one of the top fifty firms in the United States, ranked nationally at No. 10 by number of SEC clients, and ranked No. 1 in size in the Mountain Region of the United States. H&A is a high-quality accounting and auditing practice and is recognized in financial circles on a national basis. It has twenty-six partners and approximately two hundred fifty total personnel. The firm has received awards as one of the best places to work in two of its offices and was named "Best of the Best" of all accounting firms in its peer group by a national publication in 2006 and 2007.

My family was very supportive when I made the decision to leave TR&Co. and go off on my own. They understood that our future, lifestyle and livelihood would depend upon what we could accomplish in the future through our joint efforts. Melanie typed my letter of resignation, Mitch offered to go back to work to help support the family if necessary, and everyone unanimously voted no when TR&Co. called and offered me the large increase in compensation in order to persuade me to change my mind. We did not have much time to arrange our move to Denver, since the kids needed to be in school at the beginning of the school year. My former administrative assistant at TR&Co. rented a house for us sight-unseen and assured us that it would be adequate for our family in the short-term. We considered moving either back to the Cherry Hills area or to Wheat Ridge, but we ultimately decided to go to Wheat Ridge since the kids had attended school there previously. After a few months of living in the rental house, Mick, our seven-year-old, popped the question at dinner one night—"Dad, when are you going back to work?" I think the rest of the family put him up to that question, so it was time for me to move on to my new career.

In early November 1977 I met with Bill Sikora, and we decided to proceed with our partnership and start a new accounting firm in Denver, Colorado. We agreed that the new firm would be named HEIN + SIKORA and that we would start our business by the end of 1977. The Firm hereinafter is referred to H&A throughout the book. (The name was changed to HEIN + ASSOCIATES in 1982 and later to HEIN + ASSOCIATES LLP, and then to HEIN & ASSOCIATES LLP in 2004.) Bill went back to Houston and resigned from TR&Co., and we were on our way.

Our first priorities in starting H&A were to rent office space and get a bank line of credit to pay the bills. One of the large law firms at 17th and California in Denver had extra space because they had taken on a new lease and had some unneeded growth space. We rented 1,800 square feet on the thirtieth floor and had very nice space for such a new company. Getting a line of credit was another story. We went to the three largest local banks in Denver. The First National Bank of Denver wanted our business; however, they wanted collateral such as mortgages on our houses or anything else we were willing to give them. The Central Bank of Denver also wanted our business, but they wanted Certificates of Deposit as collateral. We were pretty discouraged as we had friends at both of these banks. Then we went to Colorado National Bank, where we also had friends, and they surprised us by offering us our line of credit with no collateral and no strings attached. They were willing to make the loan based on our reputations and prior business experience. Needless to say, Colorado National Bank and its successors has been H&A's bank for thirty years.

Our first days in our new office space consisted of getting started in business. We had no clients and had decided we were not going to directly contact and pursue clients of our former employers. Since we did not have any furniture or clients, we sat around on boxes containing our personal belongings and made calls to friends and business associates to stir up new business. We made a list of approximately 450 names of people that we knew, and decided that we would contact each of them for lunch, dinner or cocktails. Over the first year or so, we contacted everyone on the list. Many were willing to help us, but not a lot of people were excited about jumping on the bandwagon and becoming clients of a brand new accounting firm.

Our first tax return for calendar year 1977 indicated that H&A was started on December 15, 1977 and that its total revenues for that year were $675. The profit plan for 1978 set a goal to have revenues of three hundred thousand and to double revenues each year for the first three years. Our business strategy was to be a small boutique firm offering high-quality services to private companies. From our experience with the Big 8 accounting firms, we believed that large private companies were underserved and that there was a niche market for a high-quality local firm to serve those companies.

The executive vice president of the NYSE company, which I had worked with in Denver, called when he heard that I had left TR&Co. to start my own business. After we chatted for awhile, he told me that he was disappointed that I had not continued in the world of big corporations. After I told him that

I was committed to starting my own accounting firm and not interested in pursuing other opportunities, his final statement was, "What a waste." Several years later, when I read in the Wall Street Journal that he had retired as executive vice president of one of the largest companies in the U.S., I called him back and told him that I thought it was a "big waste" that he would retire from the corporate world at such an early age of forty-nine. He told me that he had to because he was burned out.

By the beginning of 1978, it was time to get our office ready to serve clients, assuming that we would get busy in the near term. I went to an office supply store to buy office supplies. Having been a PIC of TR&Co. offices did not prepare me for handling this activity. I bought the usual pencil, papers, folders, etc. When it came to buying the pencil sharpener, I was up against a major decision. A manual pencil sharpener was five or six dollars, and an electric pencil sharpener was seventeen dollars. After debating the pros and cons, I finally went with the manual pencil sharpener. It just did not seem like we could justify a seventeen-dollar pencil sharpener since we didn't have any clients.

I had done some reading about the economics of starting a professional services firm. According to experts, the first year would usually result in a loss, the second year should be a break-even year, and the third year should be profitable. If a profit was not achieved by the third year, it was recommended that you close your doors and go do something else. Other articles suggested that the clients of the professional services firm reflect the age of the firm. In other words, a new accounting firm can expect to get startup clients, and more mature clients would come as the firm aged. Based upon my experience with H&A, both of these concepts proved to be truer than I had hoped. We in fact had a loss in 1978 and it took many more years to get seasoned clients.

By the end of 1977, it was also time to look for a permanent residence. We decided to build a house in Genesee because the mountain environment was very appealing to us. We were the seventy-eighth building permit in that area. However, we faced one big hurdle. We had no income and were working for a new company that expected to have a loss during its first year of business. I decided to visit the executive vice president of a large savings and loan in Denver to get some advice on how to tackle this problem. Much to my surprise, he told me that he was leaving for a new job in two weeks. He said that if I would get my loan application in before he left, he was sure the loan committee would approve it since he had great faith in my ability to succeed in the future based upon my past track record. Our family was totally excited about the opportunity to build a nice house and move to the mountains. One problem with our new house was that Michelle, our two-year-old, could not walk up the slope of our driveway since she learned to walk in Houston, which is flat as a pancake.

The startup of H&A did not go as planned. Large private companies did not flock to our doors to seek our services, and the oil boom of the late 70s and early 80s was getting underway. Oil and gas clients became our mainstay, as we had significant oil and gas experience with both large and small companies. By 1981, over 80 percent of our revenues were from oil and gas companies. We had a number of oil companies resulting from IPOs that we had handled, and we had established a strong SEC niche. We also had approximately 150 investor partnerships as clients. Our large oil and gas practice could have been larger, but we did not take clients that did not have experience in the oil and gas business, and others simply did not meet our criteria. Everyone wanted to get involved in the oil and gas action. We even had one gentleman who owned a strip club in the basement of a building in Oklahoma City that wanted us to do an IPO. Needless to say, we did not take that client.

H&A was a firm with an entrepreneurial attitude, and in

some cases we invested in future IPOs rather than doing the audits. The staff of H&A was also allowed to invest in these opportunities. By the end of the oil boom, H&A had investments worth approximately $1.5 million for which the cost was about $100,000. These securities were not sold at the peak of the market for various reasons. Some had restrictions on sale for two years, others were held because of various relationships, and others were held because they looked too good to sell. The proceeds from the sale of these securities ultimately resulted in a recovery of less than the original cost.

The first four years of H&A went better than we could have expected. In the first year, our income matched expenses before partners' salaries. In the second year, our revenues doubled as we had hoped, and we generated almost enough profit to cover partners' salaries. In the third year, revenues doubled again, and we had a profit after partners' salaries. In the fourth year, revenues grew another 50 percent and the firm was quite profitable.

The early 80s in Denver, Colorado were just like the gold rush days that we have read about in books and have seen in movies. Some companies gave credit cards and cars to all of their employees, including the administrative staff. Often the party started by three o'clock in the afternoon. It was fun for a lot of people as long as it lasted.

The success of H&A in the early years was greatly facilitated by its ability to attract some extremely talented people to join a small firm to take advantage of the opportunity offered by being involved in a start-up firm. Bill Sikora ran into Bill Yeates at the Toronto Airport bar in 1979 and talked about the opportunities at H&A. Bill Yeates came to H&A and also helped entice Larry Unruh, another manager at Coopers & Lybrand, into the firm. Randy Roulier joined the firm from Pricewaterhouse and Co. because he was interested in leaving the large firm to do something more exciting with his life. Later we brought Gary

Roush to the Firm from TR&Co. and Vince Zarlengo from Ernst & Young. Obviously there were also others, but it is amazing to look back and realize that H&A was able to attract this kind of talent in its very early years.

We were also able to convince Leona Laughman to leave Houston and come to Denver to be our Director of Administration. Leona was very instrumental in helping me manage the Houston office of TR&Co., and her help and support over the many years helped H&A achieve its success. As the firm grew, our administrative functions also grew. Somewhere along the line I'm sure we bought a few electric pencil sharpeners. We also got our first word processing machine and Luanne, our great typist, used the box that it came in as her desk for several years. I think it became so comfortable that it was hard to give up when we finally got adequate facilities for the typing department.

The oil and gas boom lasted for about three years. Our business was very successful, and we held oil and gas parties at Cherry Hills Country Club. All of our clients, friends, and acquaintances in the oil and gas business attended, and some even flew in from New York City and other parts of the country. By 1980 or 1981, we were even invited by investors in New York City to open an office there to help them with their oil and gas activities. However, the oil and gas boom did not last forever. In March 1982, oil and gas prices dropped and the boom was over. By the end of 1982, no one would come to our oil and gas parties. Everybody owed everybody else money, and nobody wanted to be at a party with their creditors. Many large houses had to be sold and a lot of marriages ended in divorce. I still have good friends and great memories from the good old days, and it's fun to watch the next oil boom of the first decade of the twenty-first century.

IPOs in the oil and gas business were closing quite routinely until 1982. One of my clients that was doing an IPO was Jaclyn

Smith's father from the Midwest. His IPO went all the way through the process, but at the end the stock could not be sold by the underwriters. I believe his was the first IPO to get cancelled, signaling the beginning of the oil bust.

1982 was a significant year in the history of H&A. With the end of the oil boom in sight, Bill Sikora decided that we should pursue merger opportunities for H&A. In addition to the end of the oil and gas boom, the other partners were not comfortable with some of Bill's business attitudes. Bill Sikora's goal was to be a small boutique firm, and yet he had been very willing to make Bill Yeates, Larry Unruh, Randy Roulier, Gary Roush and Vince Zarlengo partners early in their careers. Bill Sikora's attitudes were creating conflict among the younger partners, since they obviously wanted to grow the firm as fast as possible to achieve the economic advantages of growth, whereas Bill Sikora wanted to keep the firm small and be more in control. Larry Unruh had left to seek his riches in the oil and gas business, and Randy Roulier had gone to work for an oil and gas client. After some thought, I advised Bill Sikora and the other partners that I was not interested in merging with another firm and that I was going to continue on in public accounting. Bill Yeates, Gary Roush, Vince Zarlengo, and I worked out a new business plan on a bar napkin and decided to buy Bill Sikora out.

Since 80 percent of our revenues in 1981 were from oil and gas clients, the oil bust had a significant effect on our future business. Over time most of the oil and gas business would be gone, and we would have to create new clients and opportunities for the firm in order to be successful in the future.

Family picture in our new Genesee home in 1978

The view from the deck of our Genesee home

Our Genesee home, 1978-2001

CHAPTER 8

THE REBIRTH OF H&A

The buyout agreement with Bill Sikora was signed by Bill Yeates, Vince Zarlengo, Gary Roush, and me. We had received a major break because Larry Unruh, who had had enough of the oil and gas business, agreed to come back to the firm to head the tax practice. His expertise in the oil and gas industry and structuring transactions was essential for our future success. We had a well diversified group of partners. Both Bill and Larry were from Coopers & Lybrand, Vince Zarlengo was from Ernst & Young, and Gary and I were from TR&Co. We had a good client base and had established ourselves in serving public companies. We also had joined the Securities and Exchange Commission Practice Section (SECPS) of the AICPA and had passed our peer review with flying colors in 1981. The review team appointed by the AICPA told us that H&A was the best practice that they had ever seen. Even though membership in the SECPS was not required, we had joined and volunteered to have peer reviews to ensure that our practice was high-quality and as good as we thought it was relative to our peers. Also, none of our important clients left the firm as a result of the departure of Bill Sikora. However, the 1980s were a rather turbulent time as will be obvious in reading this chapter.

The prime interest rate in the U.S. had increased from 6.25 percent in 1977 to 20.5 percent by 1981 as a result of inflation pressures caused by dramatically increasing energy prices. When oil prices decreased in the spring of 1982, the downturn in the oil and gas business and oil and gas service companies was dramatic. Some of our clients called and told us they would not be able to pay their bills, so we should not start their audits. With the departure of Bill Sikora and the tough times ahead for the oil and gas industry, I was very concerned that our little firm could experience a freefall if we did not perform services to our clients in financial trouble and were forced to lay off our staff. Therefore, we continued to do the audits and took the credit risk.

These times during the 80s were very tough. One of the most important reasons why H&A survived with such a large oil and gas client base was that we had developed quite a bit of out-of-town work because of our SEC expertise. We had a staff of fifteen people, and on some Friday evenings there were ten plane tickets on the front desk for people going out of town to provide client services. Our bankers told us that this was a general trend in Denver. Companies that had business outside of the Denver area were surviving, while those with no business outside of Denver were failing. Because of the departure of Bill Sikora, our 1982 revenues were about the same as 1981. However, we doubled our revenues during the next three years through 1985 and averaged a 27 percent compounded growth rate. We continued to get new SEC clients outside of the oil and gas industry.

During 1983, we were approached by a Houston accounting firm to consider merging with their firm to go into the Houston market, and we also brought Jack Blumenthal to the firm as a partner to start our consulting practice.

I first met Don Horton in Houston at the TR&Co. introduction party in 1977 that I attended in a sports coat, tie and slacks. Don was among those who were surprised by my attire but happy to see a change coming to Houston. During my three years in Houston, Don came to my office several times to get advice from me on how to convince one of his clients to go to a Big 8 firm, namely TR&Co. His client did not want to go to a Big 8, but was far too large for Don to do the audit since the company was planning an IPO in the $50 million range. After I left Houston, the client did go to TR&Co. and was a significant client there. One of Don's partners, an ex-TR&Co. manager, called me and asked to have lunch in Denver. The discussion included a merger of our firms. The Houston partners visited with the H&A partners, but the H&A partners were not excited about opening an office in Houston. Later that year, the H&A partners decided that the Houston merger did make sense and contacted Don Horton to reopen the merger talks. Don's partners had subsequently decided that they were not interested in the merger and that they would prefer to buy Don out of that practice and take over the firm. In later chapters, I discuss the opening of the Houston office by Don Horton when he joined our firm in 1984.

Jack Blumenthal came to H&A as a partner in 1983 from Fox & Co. He was a partner with the firm for approximately three years. Also during those three years we brought in Dennis Brown. Dennis had been a consulting partner with TR&Co. in the past. The consulting business during those three years consisted of four or five product lines. Because of the decline in the oil business, we were engaged to help several oil companies cut their internal costs. The consulting practice also included general business consulting, business valuations, business reorganization studies, and entry into the litigation support business. Our consulting revenues grew from $170,000 in its first year to $330,000 in 1984. In 1984, a new product line was launched to do the financial analysis for bond refundings by government entities. This business was kicked off based upon Jack's contacts in the investment banking community and a couple of bond refunding projects that I had worked on at TR&Co. This became a very successful product line for the firm. As the general accounting business was not that great in 1985, the profits from our bond refunding business turned what could have been a very bad year into a good year.

After the departure of Bill Sikora, various philosophies of the firm changed. Bill believed that H&A should borrow all of its capital from the bank with minimum capital contributions from partners. Also, we became a growth-oriented firm without putting any self-imposed restrictions on the growth that our partners could generate. The financial concepts for H&A were developed during this time. Based upon cash flow models that I developed, the firm created the basis for H&A's capital to be sufficient for future growth, and capital contributions and earnings distributions were predetermined. If the firm grew, our capital would automatically increase to support the growth, and earnings distributions would be based upon future earnings and predetermined distribution rates. Therefore, our firm has never had to engage in negotiations regarding the amount of capital to be contributed or the amount of earnings to be distributed.

Technological advances were occurring in the 1980s. H&A bought its first personal computer and fax machines around 1984. We also moved to new office space in 1982, and our word processor got a private area to do her work and even a nice desk. Another technology was also being developed during this time. We worked with a new client who was developing the first voice activation system. He was the engineer that developed the Cray Super Computer for Mr. Cray. This machine worked pretty well and was being tested by Montgomery Ward. Although I do not know how this technology progressed over the years to the technology used today, I suspect that the technology by this engineer was part of the basis for the development of today's sophisticated voice-activation technology.

Several economic events occurred in the 80s that had a dramatic effect on our country. The savings and loan industry was allowed to utilize very questionable accounting practices by the regulators and was also allowed to make risky investments outside the housing industry. Also, in the mid 80s a tax reform act was passed during the Reagan administration that eliminated many of the tax incentives related to the ownership of real estate.

The savings and loan companies were allowed to make loans on venture capital deals, land development plays, and other risky investments. Since deposits of S&Ls for up to $100,000 were guaranteed by the U.S. government, the S&Ls could raise significant capital guaranteed by the U.S. government and in turn invest that capital into questionable assets. The S&Ls were also allowed to use accounting practices that dramatically overstated their financial performance.

Among the poor practices by the S&Ls were the land flips occurring in Dallas, Texas. The S&Ls would loan 90 percent of appraised value on real estate and allow reappraisals every six months. Some would even advance money to the real estate companies to pay for overhead costs for them to find deals for the S&Ls to fund. The result was vast overstatements of values for real estate collateral. The appraisals always went up because companies were "flipping" land to each other at inflated prices.

The tax bill passed in the mid 80s removed the tax incentives for owning real estate, which reduced the equity in many real estate assets to zero. Assume that, on average, a real estate project would be financed 80 percent by debt and 20 percent by equity. The tax incentives caused real estate to have a higher valuation by at least 20 percent. When the incentives were removed, the investors had no more equity in many real estate projects. The real estate industry was headed for disaster.

As the real estate business deteriorated and other economic problems developed in the United States, the Resolution Trust

Corporation was formed in 1989 to bail out the savings and loan industry. Even though never described as a "bailout" of the industry by the government, many believed that the formation of the Resolution Trust was in fact a government bailout. The Resolution Trust closed 747 S&Ls and liquidated $394 billion in assets.

Personally, I tried to diversify my assets in the 1980s. I'm not exactly sure why, but it seemed like the thing to do at the time. I invested in two apartment house deals, both of which went bad. Both of those deals were with friends, which was probably a good lesson for me to learn. I also invested in two exploratory oil wells, both of which were dry holes. Exploratory wells are drilled where there are no proved reserves and are a greater risk. However, the returns are much higher with exploratory drilling when successful than with development drilling. Last but not least, I fed 400 or 500 steers over the course of five years. I never made any money at this project either, although I don't think that I lost any money either. However, my involvement in the cattle business was at least enjoyable.

During the early 1980s, H&A decided to upgrade the artwork and decorations in the office. Jane and a professional artist friend of ours took on the project. The theme was to utilize all art from Colorado artists. In addition, no CPA certificates, or other non-art hangings, were to be on the walls. The goal was to be different than other accounting firms. Each individual office had a budget for the purchase of art, and the occupant of each individual office was interviewed and allowed to be involved in the selection of their wall hangings. This was quite a unique approach to take in decorating an accounting firm's offices. At the end of the decorating project the office looked outstanding, and to celebrate, H&A had a party for all of the artists who were shown in our office. Most of them attended this celebration and were quite pleased to see their work in a local environment.

The troubling times of the 1980s were not over yet. In 1986, the president of one of our small oil and gas clients, which was owned by investors in the United Kingdom, called with some rather interesting information. He had just returned from England, where he had met with the owners of his company and the oil ambassador for Saudi Arabia. He said that he had learned at the meeting that Saudi Arabia was going to reduce the price of oil until that nation got its way with the other OPEC members. The suggestion at the meeting was that oil could go as low as nine dollars a barrel. Lo and behold, that is exactly what happened. The oil bust of 1986 basically put any remaining oil clients we had out of business or in great trouble and exacerbated the economic woes in Denver, Colorado.

One of the largest oil and gas companies in Denver was having problems and decided to seek outside investors for an investment of $100 million to shore up its capital accounts. This became one of the more interesting projects that I have been involved in, as I was asked by the potential acquirers of this company to do the due diligence for them. The investor was one of the largest banks in Europe, so it was a great thrill to see H&A engaged for this type of project. The other partners, staff, and I completed this project successfully. The investment was never made because we determined that the asking price was approximately double the real value of the company.

Because of a friend, I had moved our banking business to Cherry Creek National Bank in the mid-80s. They were heavily involved in real estate lending, and things eventually got so bad that they didn't even call us to discuss the renewal of our loan. Because of this situation, we went back to Colorado National Bank. Although our capital accounts were quite good in 1989, Colorado National Bank asked us to increase the capital of the firm. We honored this request to keep our good relations with them, which have continued for many years.

The 1980s were not only a very difficult time in Denver, Colorado, but also nationally. I am very pleased that we were able to survive the 80s and continue to build a very successful accounting firm. Although we had doubled our revenues in the three years, ending December 31, 1985, it took seven more years to double the revenues to $5 million in 1992. To all of the partners who survived the 80s, it was a great achievement for us to hit the $5 million revenue mark. During the seven years, ending December 31, 1992, we had good years in all except 1989 and 1990, which were totally flat. However, during all of the years we were a profitable firm, we continued to build our assets in terms of the expertise of the firm and the development of our people.

Backpacking into the Pintlar Wilderness Area of Montana in 1984 with Jane's sister and brother, Carol and Jerry, and Mick

Clarence and Bob Thrailkill at the annual Cherry Hills golf tournament

Clarence in London on our first European trip in 1984

Clarence and Michelle and friends with the big catch at Lake Powell

CHAPTER 9

THE FOUNDATIONS OF H&A

A major key to our success has been that the firm created an environment where people could realize their potential—both at the professional and the administrative staff levels. There are many important areas that define the business philosophies important to the success of H&A. These philosophies create a culture that is sometimes hard to define, but nevertheless has a great influence upon the direction of H&A and the careers of all of the people that have worked at the firm.

We always had a requirement that our partners have abilities in the key areas to make an accounting practice successful. These are the management of the business, the technical competence to serve clients, and the ability and desire to participate in marketing for the future growth of the firm. Not everyone has equal talents in all of these areas, but I believe that all of our partners possess strengths in each of these areas.

From day one, we had a philosophy to work hard and have fun. Our partners and wives know each other and have the ability to have fun together when the opportunity exists. In 1983, when we had survived the buyout of Bill Sikora, the partners went on a trip with their wives to Mexico to celebrate. The partners and spouses have had an annual trip ever since and have been to many nice resort destinations, including Jamaica, Hawaii, Florida, Hilton Head, and many trips to Mexico.

There are a number of rules of practice that have been part of the H&A culture since the beginning. Profit plans are developed annually with participation from offices, departments, partners, and the administrative staff. These profit plans are presented annually at the partners' meetings to keep all partners informed as to the opportunities and issues facing each office and department. The profit plans always include goals for productivity and business development, and set standards for revenues per partner.

The firm has always demanded high-quality standards from all of its people serving clients, and the technical competence to do so. The development of people has always been a key objective of the firm. The firm's success and growth is directly related to its success in this area. The firm also has standards for collections, and an accounts receivable penalty system was installed that reduced our receivables by 50 percent. This system's success was based upon two key factors. One, it was the only part of the firm that was managed in a dictatorial manner by the managing partner, and two, it made partners more responsible for their share of our business.

The firm has always emphasized excellent client service at a reasonable price. Our rates were set competitively, but not at the lowest level or at the highest level of the competition. Our client service has always emphasized involvement by partners and managers in servicing clients and utilization of experienced staff. A key part of our success has been that we deviated from the normal practice of local accounting firms. Most firms have partners servicing books of business who feel a great amount of ownership to these clients. It becomes a business where each partner has a small business within a business when operated in this manner. At H&A, we reduced the emphasis on books of business, and the ownership thereof, and assigned clients to the best personnel to provide those clients the services that they needed. This concept was essential to the future growth and success of H&A.

From day one of our partnership, we had the philosophy that partners would always take care of their fellow partners. When our partners have had major illnesses and other issues, the firm has done an outstanding job of caring for them and making difficult situations a much more tolerable experience.

Our Partnership Agreement has been a mainstay of the firm. This agreement has held up through all types of situations including opening offices, closing offices, promoting partners, terminating partners when necessary, and governing the firm in general. The agreement has standardized processes for determining capital contributions, which expand as the business grows, and making distributions in an organized manner. The agreement generally provides for payment of a portion of earnings as salaries, a portion based on ownership, and a portion for annual performance bonuses. Each partner is therefore assured of a stable income, all partners share in firm-wide earnings, and partners have a chance to earn extra money in a year where they have outstanding performance. I talk about many of the above philosophies elsewhere in this book. Even though the above areas are specific to the accounting business, many of the philosophies and guidelines are applicable to businesses of all types.

The 1984 partners' trip to Puerto Vallarta

Don Horton and Clarence with the marlin they
caught in Cabo San Lucas at the 1986 partners' trip

Annual partners' trip to Mexico

Annual partners' trip to Mexico

Jane and Clarence at a Cancun partners' trip

Annual partners' trip to Destin, Florida

Annual partners' trip to Las Vegas in 2003

CHAPTER 10

H & A GROWS UP

The Denver office added some key personnel in the 80s who became partners and have played an important role in the development of our practice. Mira Finé and Greg Dickey came to the firm in the mid-80s and have been instrumental in creating our tax practice. Jim Brendel and Brian Mandell-Rice joined the firm in 1987 and are leaders in our audit practice. Wayne Gray joined the Denver office in the 80s, transferred to Dallas in 1987, and has been the PIC of that office for twenty years. Rich Anderson was also hired in Denver and transferred to Houston. As I will discuss later, Rich was a key part of developing our Houston office. Dennis Brown, who came to the firm as a partner, played an important role in the development of our litigation support practice.

In 1983, beginning with the concept of a Houston office, I began to become restless and decided that I would like to try to build a big firm as opposed to operating in a small local firm environment. I got my wish when we opened Houston in 1984, Dallas in 1987, and Southern California in 1993. During this process, there were times when I had forty trips on my schedule on January 1st of each year. On top of that, there were always other trips related to specific business events. I estimate that I flew more than two million miles during my career with H&A.

The Houston office opened in 1984 when the oil and gas industry was having its difficulties. Houston is a very energy-based economy, so times were tough. Things did not improve as the oil and gas business and the related service industry experienced even further decline from the 1986 oil bust. We started from scratch, since Don Horton had sold his prior practice to his former partners with covenants that he would not take any of his clients back. Times were so difficult that Don offered, on occasion, to close the office if the firm felt like the battle was going to be too tough to win.

Don Horton's former partners lost their biggest client, which was very significant to their practice, shortly after they bought Don out. This client was in Tyler, Texas, and had gone with KPMG for a year or so when they decided that it was time to make another change. Don and I went out to Tyler to talk to the principal about making the change from KPMG to H&A. He was quite an impressive financier who had put together oil and gas interests, savings and loans, banks, and other interests. During that meeting, he tested my business judgment a little and also expressed his displeasure at Don having sold his business to his partners. After several hours he became comfortable with us and gave us all of his business. The annual fees were approximately $500,000, which was enough to make the Houston office very successful. Business is filled with surprises, however, and we received one the next morning. The Tyler financier had passed away that night and his business affairs became uncertain. Even though this was a business loss, it was also a sad time for us because Don and he had been very good friends for many years.

The Houston office became profitable in 1986 after suffering small losses in 1984 and 1985. Despite all of the difficulties, we were on the road to success in Houston. In 1987, the Houston office obtained a large client from a referral in London, England. This client was too good to be true. They paid their bills on time without question and seemed to be on the way to being a very successful insurance enterprise. Before the end of the audit, however, we had some serious questions about the investments being made by the company. There were also under-the-table rumors that some of the executives may have had legal issues in the past. We worked hard to validate the investments and hired a national detective agency to check out the background of the principals. The background checks came back clean, and investments were certified by a major U.S. investment bank. After we began the next year's audit, the investments held by the company grew more questionable and rumors continued about the background of the executives. Some of the audit evidence came back and looked improper, and we were finally able, through another detective agency, to determine that some of the executives did in fact have legal issues. After we resigned from the account, one of the principals called and threatened to sue me because he had heard that I was slandering his name and that I had made the comment to someone that he had been convicted of securities fraud. He strongly objected, since he had only been convicted of mail fraud.

During the early years of the Houston office, we had turnover in our audit partners and Rich Anderson left the firm to go to work for a seismic company. The audit practice was suffering from lack of leadership and an effective audit partner. While reviewing resumes we had received over a year or so, I came across the resume of Keith Tunnell, who was an audit manager with KPMG in the eastern U.S. Keith was hired into the firm in 1991 and discovered that the audit practice was smaller than he had originally thought and was, in fact, in poor shape. Keith called every audit client and asked them to give him a second chance. He also told them that he would commit to providing outstanding audit service in the future. The rest is history; Keith turned the audit practice around and made it very successful.

Rich Anderson returned to the firm, and he, Keith, and

Don continued to build the office. When Don retired in 1995, Keith and Rich rotated the PIC responsibilities with Rich going first and Keith second. This was because Don, Keith and Rich decided that both Rich and Keith should give it a try to see which one liked it. Both of them enjoyed it very much, and ultimately the office selected Keith to be the permanent PIC. Rich ultimately left the firm and is now a very successful oil man in Houston. Kenny Grace joined the firm as a partner early in 1997, is a Houston native, and is very instrumental in the success of the office.

I enjoyed developing the Houston office and working with Don Horton and many other people in Texas very much. I have always enjoyed my travels there because of the years I had spent in Houston and my ability to retain some long-term friendships. The first two years of 1984 and 1985 were filled with significant efforts to attract new clients and grow the office. Don and I and others spent two days a month having breakfast, lunch, dinner, and cocktails with everybody we knew in order to get the office up and running in a tough environment.

The Dallas office was started in 1987 in part to be closer to East Texas, where we had some clients and a lot of contacts. We started the office with a former TR&Co. tax supervisor who had built up a small tax practice. Wayne Gray transferred from the Denver office to Dallas shortly after we opened it to take care of the audit practice that we had and to develop the office. The tax supervisor that we had brought in to start the office had the option, as is usual, to stay or leave the firm after one year. Even though the business was getting off the ground, he decided that he would leave. Our firm philosophy was to hire people and then go out and get the business. This was the operating mode of the Denver office when we hired talented people whenever they became available. We never had the business before bringing in the people. The reason the tax supervisor we had brought in to start the Dallas practice left was that he could never get comfortable with the idea of hiring people first before we got the business. He decided to go back to his old lifestyle of having a small firm consisting of him and his secretary. Wayne took over as PIC of the office, and over the years we developed a successful practice. Megan McFarland moved to Dallas later and became a key partner in the office. Megan's move to Dallas coincides with the period when that office started experiencing better growth. Whenever I called the Dallas office and Megan answered the phone, I would ask her what she was doing because the office seemed to be getting more new business and growing. Megan always would giggle and act like she didn't know the reason for the newfound success of the office.

The SoCal office was opened in 1993 with John Steinbeck. John was coming to us from another local firm; he had no employees, and a limited amount of business. The SoCal office was opened because the L.A. area always seemed to have a significant amount of business synergism with Denver. I don't think we have any idea why this was the case; however, we had significant business opportunities in the area all through the 80s. I recall that we worked on at least fourteen different client projects in that area before opening the office. I ran many ads in our quest to open an office. Over time, I talked to and interviewed approximately eighty people who were interested in the opportunity to join our firm. One day, after having about given up on the idea of finding anyone to open the office, I re-reviewed the resumes that I had. John's resume looked interesting since he had Big 8 experience and had SEC experience, which was compatible with H&A. When I called John to talk to him, he was quite surprised. He had sent his resume in approximately six months before I called and had assumed that he would not receive a call. He told me that he was working in his garage when the call came and was a little unprepared for his initial telephone interview.

The SoCal office was basically a break-even operation for the first three years. By 1996 and 1997, the office was profitable and by 1998, very successful. During this growth period, John called me one day and said that he was rather disappointed because the number of clients that he was expecting to be generated by the H&A contacts was not materializing. All of this was true and somewhat surprising to me also. I told John to have some patience because it could take longer than we originally thought to achieve the expected synergism. The synergism did occur then big-time. After that, there were years when the Denver/H&A contacts produced over $2 million a year of business for the SoCal office.

Scott Appel joined the SoCal office from relationships he developed with the Denver office in the mid-90s. Scott made a strong commitment to the firm to help us develop the office, made partner, and became PIC of that office in 2008. Ralph Kuhen saw an ad in a newspaper in Southern California in 2000, and was so impressed with the ad that he called the firm to see if he could become a member of H&A. Ralph had sold his practice in another city and decided it was time to go back into public accounting.

John Steinbeck developed personal problems and ultimately was not able to continue with the firm. He passed away as a very young man. Ralph Kuhen replaced John as the PIC of the office in 2002 and, with Scott's help, turned the office around and enabled us to continue our practice in SoCal.

In 1986, a major event occurred that would help propel H&A to its future growth and success. Moores Rowland International (MRI) contacted the firm and invited us to join their international association. MRI was being reorganized because their national associate in the United States had merged with another firm. My recollection is that we were the sixth firm to join the new network of MRI. Initially, there were two benefits to H&A for being involved in an international network. One was the ability to market international capabilities to service clients.

The world was already moving to the international stage, and I believed it was important for us to have these capabilities. The second benefit was that it afforded the ability to make great trips. The U.S. firms met twice annually in the U.S., including one in Naples, Florida. In addition, the international firms also met every year. They were the only international association that had annual partners' meetings of all firms. This enabled me to take some great trips and see the world. Other partners in the firm also made some international trips as a result of the association. Don Horton and Wayne Gray accompanied me to several international meetings. Bill Yeates went to Singapore, China and other destinations. Jim Brendel served as the audit partner for an Italian company and made trips to Italy. As time went on, Larry Unruh and others also took over the travel because I was tired of travel and flying around in airplanes.

Shortly after joining MRI, I managed to get elected to the executive board of MRI. The executive board met in connection with the European MRI meetings and during the international meetings. Therefore, I went to Europe every year for the executive board meeting and also attended the board meetings during the international meetings. I served on the board for six years, so I was able to see twelve or thirteen countries that I would never have been able to visit without the MRI connection.

Ultimately the biggest benefit of belonging to MRI was the ability to associate with a peer group of firms and compare financial information and business efforts. These comparisons led to setting higher achievable goals and raised the expectations of H&A significantly. Just as an example, a comparison of revenues per partner and earnings per partner caused us to set higher goals. In every case, our partners and the firm were able to step up to the new standards.

Our association with MRI also helped strengthen my belief that a bright future existed for the growth and development of regional firms to provide a higher level of service to small and medium-sized companies. Most regional and smaller national firms had been merged into the Big 8 accounting firms, leaving a void in the marketplace. The H&A partners had a number of discussions regarding the benefits of becoming a regional firm vs. staying a local firm and the risks and costs of developing multiple offices. The firm's ability to serve its clients and the success of its practice has been very satisfying.

As previously mentioned, H&A joined the SECPS in 1980. The SECPS was formed in 1977 to enhance the audit quality of all accounting firms serving public companies. The SECPS was supervised by the Public Oversight Board (POB), which had five members who are not members of the profession. Members included Arthur Wood, former Chairman and CEO of Sears, Roebuck and Company, and Melvin Laird, former Secretary of Defense. I volunteered to be a peer reviewer for the third peer review ever performed by the SECPS. This was in Tampa, Florida in 1980. Membership in the SECPS was voluntary until 1990, when the rules changed and accounting firms serving SEC clients were required to become members and subject themselves to the SECPS peer reviews. H&A had its first peer review in 1981 and has had these reviews throughout its history.

The accounting profession managed its participation in the SECPS by an executive committee (SECPSEC). The SECPSEC consisted of all national firms and the number of smaller firms that would be equal to one less than the number of national firms. This was to ensure that the national firms always had control of the committee. I volunteered to serve on the SECPSEC and was a member of the executive board from 1985 to 2003. That was easily the longest term of anyone on the committee. There were twenty-one members when I first started on the committee, and by the time my involvement ended, the committee consisted of seven national firms and six smaller firms.

For four years I also served on the planning committee, which was the executive committee of the SECPSEC. That committee consisted of five members and was responsible for planning meetings and setting priorities for actions on behalf of the entire SECPS, much like a corporate executive committee. During the initial years, the SECPSEC met four times a year and in later years met three times a year. When I was on the planning committee, I also attended four planning committee meetings on an annual basis. As a result, from 1985 to 2003, I flew to New York for these meetings from as little as three times a year to as many as ten times a year. I eventually felt like New York had become a second home.

It was quite an experience to be involved with the SECPSEC and attend the meetings with the large firms. I recall one meeting at the AICPA offices in New York where the Big 8 firms were gathered to talk about ways to quit low-ball bidding each other and stop acting in a nonprofessional manner, while in the next meeting room the Federal Trade Commission was meeting to develop rules requiring that there be more competition among the accounting firms.

In my entire career in public accounting spanning forty-two years, it always seemed to me that the accounting profession had a powerful desire to meet public expectations and to maintain high quality in their work. In my eighteen years of being involved with the SECPSEC, my respect for the profession grew, since there was never an event that occurred that caused the profession to not operate in the most professional manner possible. Obviously there are always individual failures, and the profession suffered from fast growth and the difficulties of performing audits of increasingly complex worldwide business organizations.

The SEC is an outstanding government agency and, in my opinion, the best in Washington, D.C. Over the years, the SEC saw what they considered too many instances of a lack of adequate performance by the accounting profession. The SEC's attitude towards business in general and the profession became more and more adversarial. The relationship between the SEC and the profession deteriorated to the point where meetings between the accounting profession and the SEC were less than cordial. In approximately 2001, a new chief accountant for the SEC was named. When we had meetings with SEC personnel, he required that all SEC staff shake hands with the members of the accounting profession. In the case of H&A in the early years, the SEC was very friendly and sympathetic to us and to small-firm issues. It was very clear, however, that as time went on, our relationship with the SEC also changed—as it did with the entire business community.

The SECPS was the profession's last chance to maintain control of the accounting and auditing business in the private sector. During my career beginning in the '60s, it seems like every ten years there was an effort to regulate the profession and transfer control to a quasi-government entity. The profession managed to maintain control of accounting and auditing in the private sector until the collapse of Enron in 2001. In 2002, the U.S. Senate unanimously passed the Sarbanes-Oxley Act. The auditing business was now a regulated industry.

Clarence runs the Bolder Boulder in 1987

Jane on our surprise twenty-fifth anniversary trip to the
British Virgin Islands

Mick and Clarence fish the Black Canyon in Colorado in 1994

Our home in the British Virgin Islands on a five-day sail

CHAPTER 11

THE KEYS TO A SUCCESSFUL ACCOUNTING FIRM

During the 1970s, I developed the belief that there were six key elements to developing and growing an accounting firm. Over the thirty-three years that I was involved in the management of accounting practices, these key ingredients to success never changed. I presented these criteria several times to national training meetings focusing on management of accounting firms. The six keys to success are: practice development, people development, client service, profitability, quality, and a one-firm attitude. The managers of an accounting firm must be able to execute all six of these goals simultaneously to maximize their success. I have often heard managers of accounting firms say that if they are expected to make money, they should not be expected to develop people and sell new business at the same time. Accounting firms led by managers with those attitudes and abilities generally will not excel. One large member of our MRI association engaged a consulting firm to develop the management keys to measure performance for their firm. The consulting fee was $300,000 and the product was quite detailed and impressive. However, the consulting firm left off the criteria of quality and a one-firm attitude. So even though their consulting report covered the other areas in greater detail than I would utilize, quality is a keystone of a successful professional firm and must be considered a key element for success. A one-firm attitude is also critical to develop a firm with multiple geographical areas of business and with multi-product lines.

At H&A, we developed annual profit plans for the entire firm, each individual office, and each department. Each partner in the firm was asked to set personal goals in the six areas discussed above. The partners' individual goals could be reconciled with the office and departmental goals so that all pieces of the puzzle would fit into the total firm goals. On a monthly basis, all partners received a one-page status report showing the comparison of actual performance for the total firm, office, departments, and individual partners relative to their goals for the year. Everyone in the firm could quickly see how H&A was doing and could see how each piece of the puzzle was doing relative to their annual goals. Some of the specific areas that relate to the six keys to success are discussed below.

Practice development is the key to growing and developing an accounting firm. Without developing new business, the firm would decline in size rather than grow because clients often merge, sell out, and sometimes simply do not survive. At H&A, we set new business goals for offices, departments, and individual partners. The total of these goals equaled the new business that we believed would be required to meet our profit plans that set our overall growth objective for the total firm. New business goals not only included new clients, but also additional services to existing clients and non-recurring services for special projects. Individual goals for practice development also included specific areas such as community development and the development of industry niches such as the oil and gas industry and our SEC reporting practice.

People development is probably the most important aspect to developing a successful accounting firm. For an accounting firm or other business, their most important assets walk in the front door in the morning and out the door in the evening. In an accounting firm, some offices and departments seem to have the ability to develop people so successfully that they can transfer people to other business units. That ability to me is the ultimate measure of a success in the area of people development. People develop in accounting firms through formal annual training programs that are required by the profession, as well as additional training provided by the firm. However, most of the development of technical and other skills required to be successful are learned through experience in working with clients. At H&A, our personnel enjoy a very challenging professional experience because of the diversity and complexity of the services provided by the firm. Our administrative personnel are certainly challenged to keep up with the growth of the firm and the many challenges of implementing new systems and procedures for all aspects of our business.

Client service is critical to developing an accounting firm. Several times throughout the years, H&A has completed studies to determine the source of new clients for the firm. Approximately 70 percent of all new clients come from referral sources, and without these referrals, obviously we would not be able to meet our growth objectives. Part of evaluating success with client service is to monitor lost clients on an annual basis, as well as to monitor client satisfaction from personal contact. H&A discussed doing client satisfaction surveys, since many firms undertake this process. H&A did complete an extensive client satisfaction survey and utilized appropriate procedures through an outside statistical firm. However, even though well-designed, clients were reluctant to provide candid information that would evaluate client service in depth. Another criteria we used in measuring client service was the amount of client billing volume for the partners. H&A increased the expected volumes periodically based upon industry financial surveys and financial surveys done by the MRI member firms. Keeping up with industry standards was a little uncomfortable for many of us, but we always seemed to be able to set our sights higher and to quickly rise to those levels and achieve the new goals.

Profitability is an important aspect of doing business. Businesses that are not profitable have a very short lifespan. As a young man, someone told me that there were only two things that were important to watch in an accounting firm in order to make money. One was utilization, or the level of chargeability of the staff, and the other was allowances, which measures the amount of collections to be realized from the services provided. Although this philosophy is true to some extent, the accounting business is a bit more complex than that, and I believe it is critical to achieve success in each of the six areas.

At H&A, we monitored our volume of business, utilization or productivity, allowances, and accounts receivable collections by office, department, and individual partner. I always paid attention to our volume of business and accounts receivable collections because someone else told me that the only way an accounting firm could go broke was if it had too many leases and/or was unable to collect its bills.

The quality of our work was of tremendous importance to H&A. Quality includes the technical competence to perform the services needed to serve our clients; the ability to improve on the accounting, tax, and audit performance for engagements; the desire to recognize and anticipate special needs of our clients; the ability to provide services for complex transactions; the ability to appropriately deal with circumstances that pose risks to our firm and the public; and the desire to attract good clients and resign from clients that do not meet our risk and ethical standards. The complexity of our practice, because of SEC reporting and our involvement in complex financial transactions, required us to be cognizant of the risks faced by accounting firms from the U.S. Judicial system. We demanded very high integrity from all of our personnel and from all of our clients. Most people that came to work at H&A could not believe the firm's requirements for accepting and retaining clients. We only accepted clients that met our standards, and we did not retain clients that did not meet them. The three standards that we always required were that the company had a realistic business plan and product, that management was of high integrity, and that the company had the financial resources to have a reasonable chance of success.

The technical ability of all of our professional staff ultimately became the key factor in the quality of the firm. This technical ability was constantly monitored and improved upon. In addition, we monitored the ability of our partners and staff to manage firm risk. H&A has always supported its professional staff when making tough decisions with respect to issues faced by our clients. We also joined the SECPS and had voluntary peer reviews every three years during its existence. These peer reviews were viewed as a method to improve the quality of our firm. Accounting firms are subject to significant litigation risk in the United States. At one time, the Big 8 accounting firms had lawsuits of $2.5 trillion pending against them. H&A has only had one serious lawsuit filed against it during my career. We performed the audit for a company that had completed an IPO and then went into bankruptcy a year or so thereafter. The company's failure was due to the fact that it grew too fast and mismanaged its affairs after the IPO. The audit of H&A showed no deficiencies, but lawsuits are typically filed against accounting firms because of their deep pockets. This lawsuit was settled for a reasonable amount, considering the cost of future litigation and the risks associated with going to trial.

The one-firm attitude is very important to achieve success in an accounting firm, especially with multiple locations and departments. All businesses go through cycles and need the support of the organization to achieve success over the years. Most importantly, success is achieved by the assistance that the offices, departments, and partners receive from others within the firm when needed. In the complex world we all live in, sharing the knowledge and abilities of the individual members enables H&A to provide outstanding services to a wide variety of complex clients and special projects.

The ability of H&A, and each of its partners, to execute in all of the above areas simultaneously has allowed the firm to grow, develop, and achieve its goals.

CHAPTER 12

THE MATURATION OF H&A

It took eleven years for me to consider H&A to be a stable company. At that point, I felt that the firm had strong people, a good client base, and a strong enough financial position to withstand the peaks and valleys of future business events. Our partner group formed a strong core to move forward into the future. The Houston office was established and profitable, and the Dallas office was ready to move forward.

H&A's revenue grew at a very nice pace throughout its existence, even though there were a few exceptions along the route. After achieving the landmark revenue base of $5 million in 1992, the firm doubled to $10 million in 1997, doubled again to $20 million in 2001, and doubled again to $40 million in 2006. The firm's growth rates were among the best in the country because all of our growth was achieved without doing any mergers or acquisitions of other accounting firms.

My schedule during the growth and development of H&A was very busy with diverse activities. Because of the demands of my schedule, seven-day workweeks were not uncommon. I read all SEC reports for clients with which the firm was involved, provided litigation support and business valuation services and other special projects, opened and supported each of the offices including monthly visits to support their activities, served as audit partner for numerous clients, and served on five boards of directors simultaneously.

I served on the SECPSEC and its planning committee from 1985 to 2003, was a founding board member for the Colorado Business Committee for the Arts, served on the Finance Committee for Cherry Hills Country Club, and served as a Director and Treasurer of the Genesee Fire Department. I was a board member and chairman of the audit committee for Electromedics, Inc., a medical equipment manufacturer, and a board member and chairman of the audit committee of Ultimate Electronics, Inc., a $750 million electronics retailer. Electromedics was sold to Metronics, a large international company, for $100 million. The sale of a public company in the United States is a very interesting experience. Once an offer is received, competing bids must be accepted from other potential buyers, even though the initial agreements state that the company will not solicit other buyers. Large breakup fees are included in the agreements in case higher bids are received. Without going through this process, the officers and directors of a public company can be subjected to litigation for damages for not selling the company to the highest bidder. In the case of Electromedics, higher bids were received, and the purchase price was increased significantly by this process. So in this case, the system worked. Serving as Director and Treasurer of the Genesee Fire Department was also challenging, interesting, and fun. I was able to help them fully fund their pension plan and acquire funds to purchase new fire trucks and upgrade the fire station.

Jane and the kids did get some rewards for putting up with all of my hard work and travel. My service on the MRI Executive Committee resulted in many overseas trips. Jane accompanied me on many of those, and our entire family went to the meeting in Vienna in 1987, allowing us to tour several countries by automobile. The major news headline during this trip was the stock market crash of 1987. I also took each of the kids to New York on an individual basis, and since I had probably made over 150 trips to New York, I was a good tour director. They got to see most of the important sights, as well as attend some of my meetings with me.

One of the activities I used to develop and expand H&A's recognition in the financial community was to meet with underwriters on my many trips to New York. I would arrange these meetings through introductions from clients and other contacts within the firm. Other partners also accompanied me on some of these trips to introduce their offices to the financial community. Developing contacts within the investment banking community turned out to be a very difficult proposition. The turnover in the investment banking firms makes it difficult to develop a relationship with any particular one. However, as these bankers moved around, the relationships developed helped us expand our reputation, retain clients, and obtain new business.

During my career in public accounting, it always seemed to me that the most prestigious and successful accounting firms provided extended services to their clients beyond the traditional accounting and auditing work. The successful firms had strong tax departments and generally provided management consulting services. H&A has been successful in developing non-traditional services. The firm has SEC credentials, a sophisticated tax practice, and has been successful in providing litigation support services. The firm provided information technology services from the mid-90s until 2003 and had a general consulting practice from 1998 to 2001. Even though we gave those businesses the good old college try, our experience was similar to most smaller accounting firms...it is difficult to develop a general consulting practice in smaller firms.

I was also involved in providing litigation support for approximately forty litigation cases and for probably as many business valuation cases throughout my career with H&A. This work is very stressful, requires significant time commitments on a short-notice basis, and is extremely challenging. I spent about 10 percent of my time over the years involved in these types of projects. This work is very profitable and has other benefits, such as increasing the firm's image in the legal community.

One of the cases that I worked on lasted four to five years. On behalf of the plaintiffs, I provided extensive consulting services for an insolvency case in connection with a leverage buyout transaction. The lawsuit involved several hundreds of millions of dollars and required an extensive analysis of insolvency matters and business valuations. Accounting standards did not exist for insolvency cases, so the attorneys told me to forget everything I knew about accounting and create insolvency accounting standards that would be accepted by the courts in the United States. I made adjustments to the subject company's net worth, totaling $1 billion, and testified that the company was insolvent. These were amazing numbers, considering that I complained in college that the accounting problems presented had questions involving companies with a million dollars in sales. I thought it was pretty silly at the time to be working with such large numbers, since I never expected to see a company that large.

I worked on another case involving a multibillion-dollar British company. The company claimed damages for a loss due to a theft of inventory items from a South African mine. In this case, I was required to analyze worldwide transactions for precious gem inventories that were recorded in five different currencies and several quality and weight measurements. During this work, I had to convert every transaction for fifteen years into U.S. dollars and kilos to provide standardized comparisons from which to analyze the business activities.

I also worked on another case involving insolvency defending the officers, owners, and directors of a large national health club chain against claims of $150 million. This litigation required the valuation of numerous business entities, insolvency issues, and accountants' malpractice.

During the oil boom of the early 1980s, many oil and gas investments in various oil and gas limited partnerships were sold under questionable circumstances, and I was engaged to work on one of the largest fraud cases during this timeframe. It involved claims of fraud by the plaintiffs who had invested approximately $150 million in various oil and gas partnerships. This litigation involved lender liability issues and the calculation of damages regarding the sale of partnership interests against the oil and gas general partner and the Federal Deposit Insurance Corporation. This litigation also involved accountants' malpractice claims against the auditors of the general partner.

I also worked on a very difficult litigation matter involving an international actuarial firm. This case required an analysis of insurance company rate-setting and accounting practices. The insurance company claimed damages of $30 million from the actuarial firm for professional malpractice. This case was one that was very disappointing in many respects. The insurance company really had suffered no damages as a result of the actuarial firm; however, they sued the actuarial firm to see what they could get out of the case. This was a situation where the insurance company received a settlement primarily because the actuarial firm did not feel it was in their best interest to take the risk of presenting such a complex case regarding actuarial calculations of rates and other matters to a jury. I can say that in all of the cases that I had worked on that were ultimately decided by juries, the juries generally come up with the right answers. However, there are many complex cases where the risk of a jury settlement is too great to try the case.

The most satisfying case that I worked on was serving as a special master involving a shareholder dispute for a company with diversified business interests. Because of the complex financial matters involved, both sides agreed to use a special master to issue a report to determine the effect of numerous transactions. A special master is essentially both a judge and a jury. The special master's report is used to resolve the case, and both parties agree to accept the results. The special master has the ability to request information as needed to make the findings. In this case, the dispute was largely caused by a complete lack of facts to resolve the issues. After working on this case for awhile and realizing the impossibility of analyzing the piles of data that had been accumulating, I asked for the auditor's work papers, which still existed. These audit work papers laid out and reconciled all the transactions, and I was able to issue a report resolving the case. The defendant in this case was being sued for $3 million and as a result of my report received $2 million, as opposed to paying out the $3 million.

In the middle of our years of growth and prosperity, 1995 was destined to be an exception. H&A was very transaction-oriented, and our clients were inactive in doing business transactions in 1995. In addition, some of our major clients experienced difficulties, and the net result was that our revenues declined 13 percent. This was such a tough year that I deviated from my normal compensation policies of paying bonuses for those partners that managed to have a good year. Instead, we all shared earnings based upon our ownership percentage, and everyone shared in the difficulties experienced that year. Fortunately, this was a one-time event and everyone survived. As is obvious from our numbers, the firm continued to grow and excel in future years.

One of our clients in 1995 that was experiencing difficulties was a large software company. The company had serious financial-reporting issues that came to light during our audit. They had difficulty closing their books on time, and the audit team became quite concerned because reporting revenue for software companies is a difficult issue in any case. We refused to start our audit until the company was able to close its books and record its transactions. After we started the audit, a sales executive disclosed to one of our staff that there were concerns about some of the company's activities in recording sales. Eventually we discovered through our audit that there were reporting issues with respect to a substantial number of software sales. The underwriters for the company came to Denver and asked us to retain the account. They said they would do whatever it would take for us to stay. We told them to investigate and fix the problems, and that we would then look at the company as a new client and accept them only if they met our criteria. These types of situations are among the most difficult for the CPA. By doing the right thing, which is required, the result is a disaster. The company ended up going out of business and many of the officers faced severe legal consequences.

Another fraud situation that was quite alarming to me occurred several years later. I was asked to attend a meeting with the controller of a small Denver public company and her attorney. Some concerns had been expressed regarding the recording of various sales transactions. At the meeting, the controller shocked both the attorney and I when, in response to a question about other possible issues, she disclosed that she, at the company's request, had been cooking the books for a number of years. A substantial portion of the company's assets did not exist and had been recorded to allow the company to report profits on a quarterly basis. This accounting fraud was so massive that I recommended that the controller disclose this to the board of directors. The attorneys agreed, and we went with her to the board to directors to help her make this disclosure. This is what you call a bad hair day for the directors, because they were totally blown away when they found out that most of their assets didn't exist as a result of a massive accounting fraud. Needless to say, there were some major criminal proceedings as a result of these activities.

Another fraud situation came to light about this same time

in Los Angeles. We were hired by Denver attorneys with the consent of the SEC to do an audit of an oil and gas promoter who had raised $160 million from investors. H&A personnel had visited the Company and were concerned about the records to audit. I travelled there a couple of weeks later to take a look for myself. The company presented me with a small box of bank statements and several pages of listings of bank transactions. When they contended that this was all of their records for twelve public limited partnerships and the bank showed a balance of several hundred dollars, I realized that there indeed was a massive fraud (Ponzi-scheme) involved. Fearing for my life, I left for the day to return the next day with other H&A personnel to copy records to prove the fraud. I turned these records over to the attorneys and went back to Denver. Criminal charges resulted for the principals.

1999 was a year of change for H&A. We created a national office and purchased a new accounting software system. Charlene Willey was hired as National Director of Marketing, Kay Moore was hired as Director of Human Resources, and Robin Demko was hired as our Controller. Kay Moore wrote our Employee Manual before passing away unexpectedly. Robin Demko installed our accounting system, which I will discuss further below. Robin was killed in 2005 in a tragic car accident after moving her two young children to Durango, Colorado to provide a small-town life for them.

At the time, there were no standardized software packages for regional accounting firms that would allow for the interactive processing of transactions among multiple offices and departments. Therefore, H&A decided to purchase the CMS software package that had been developed primarily for attorneys but was being marketed to accounting firms. Prior to H&A, I believe there were only three or four other accounting firms that had installed this software. This implementation was quite a major undertaking for the firm. Eventually, after

136

considering various alternatives, I became the project manager, Robin performed all the work to install the system, and one of our IT employees provided the technical assistance. One of the MRI firms that had installed this software spent $4.5 million for the installation process. Robin and I started the project in March 1999, and it went live in September 1999. I don't know what the total cost of this system was, but Robin, the IT person on a part-time basis, and several other part-time employees managed to get the job done. When we finished this project, one of the few things that I knew about in my life for sure was that I would never be the project manager for a software installation again. Looking back, I am still astounded that we were able to get this project completed. I will be forever grateful to Robin, who pulled off a minor miracle for the firm. Even though she had just started with the firm and had never worked for an accounting firm, she was willing to make an incredible personal sacrifice to get the job done. I would often go back to meet with Robin at nine or ten at night to give her insight as to the specific needs of H&A with respect to developing the software programs and reports.

In 2001, H&A implemented its first Rainmakers program that was developed for the Firm by a consulting group. This program requires three years to complete and provides training for partners, managers, and supervisors in sales, staff-training, and other business skills. The program requires three offsite meetings each year and a large time and dollar commitment. The program was expected to directly affect new business, improve office interaction, improve staff retention, and lower turnover. All of these goals were achieved to a far greater extent than we had hoped, and we have many new talented partners whose careers were enhanced by Rainmakers. It took some effort on my part and Charlene Willey to keep the program going forward, but after a year or so everyone realized that the costs and effort required were well worth it.

The tech industry bust of 2000 was the biggest fraud ever perpetrated by Wall Street. When the bubble burst it was hard to tell what the total losses to our economy were; however, I've always believed that it was in the range of trillions rather than billions. The NASDAQ stock market exceeded $5,000, and based upon historical standards, it should only have been priced at around $1,500. Cisco Systems was selling at fifty times its earnings projected five years out. Wall Street was taking start-up companies public for up to $150 million based upon a paper business plan. After these companies became public, they started buying computer software and equipment to build their infrastructures. The computer manufacturers were happy to sell them these products and sometimes invested in the small companies, further pumping up their stock. Most of these companies did not succeed, so in effect, the sales of the large computer companies were one-time non-recurring sales. The earnings and multiples were being driven up by sales that would not likely occur in the future. H&A never pursued the public offerings related to this technology boom. It was obvious to us that the whole thing was going to collapse and that litigation would result taking years to resolve.

H&A also looked at opening other offices over the years. In the late 1990s, we looked at opening an office in San Jose, California. The firm had some large clients there and the marketplace looked appealing. I met with a number of firms in the area and found that there were no non-Big 6 firms (two of the Big 8 had merged into other firms) doing any audits in San Jose. The market there seemed right for a firm like ours who could handle public companies and provide competition in the audit business. We made an offer to a firm in the area and considered moving Brian Mandell-Rice to San Jose to start an office from scratch. At the end of the day, we did not open this office, which turned out to be the best of all worlds since the economy in the Silicone Valley collapsed in 2000. We also looked at opening an office in Phoenix in the late 1990s and eventually opened a small office. This was the only time H&A did an acquisition. The office was eventually merged into another accounting firm several years later because the Phoenix market did not develop as we had initially planned.

In 2001, H&A began developing its succession plan to replace me as the managing partner. I would turn sixty-five in the year 2004 and would retire under our mandatory retirement requirements of the partnership agreement. When we began the succession plan process, there was some concern by my possible replacements that I would be a hard act to follow, since the firm was performing so well. However, 2002 turned out to be a flat year, which made it a little easier on my successor to move forward in the future.

The Sarbanes-Oxley Act was passed in 2002 by Congress. On the negative side of the Act, the audit profession in the United States became a regulated industry. On the positive side, however, the Act provided tremendous opportunity for firms such as H&A to obtain tax and consulting work from bigger companies that could no longer be provided by the Big 4 accounting firms (another firm merged and Arthur Andersen went out of business). During my last year before retirement from H&A, I revised the firm's quality control documents and auditing procedures to comply with the Sarbanes-Oxley Act. The potential for the firm as a result of this Act seemed unlimited, but the idea of being regulated by the U.S. government was not very appealing.

Michelle and Melanie in the Sound of Music
Carousel in Salzburg, Austria

Clarence and some Australian MRI partners
in 1988 meeting in Sydney

The Hein family going to a concert in Salzburg

Jane at Picton, New Zealand in 1988

Clarence planning travel in Amsterdam

Jane and Clarence going to the Captain's Ball
on the Queen Elizabeth 2

Tikal, the Mayan capital in Guatemala,
which we visited from Belize

Clarence and the Executive Committee of MRI
in Hong Kong in 1993

Jane and Clarence in Oregon in 1999

Clarence in Miami

Clarence with Dick Geiermann and Jim Simmons
at his sixtieth birthday party at Cherry Hills

Clarence snorkeling in Grand Cayman in 1994

The Hein family in Belize to become certified scuba divers in 1992

Clarence at the beach bar in Abaco to watch
the Broncos playoff game in 1999

Clarence fly-fishing

Clarence duck hunting

Clarence skiing, 1988

Clarence fishing the Big Horn River in Montana

CHAPTER 13

THE SUCCESSION PLAN

The retirement of a founder of an accounting firm is quite often a difficult process. I was recently interviewed by a person who is planning to write future articles, and possibly even a book, about the difficulties of creating an adequate succession plan for the retirement of the founders. This person indicated that my retirement, and the succession to new management of H&A, was one of the most successful that she had ever seen. The succession plan for H&A was developed very early, probably even at the very beginning of H&A.

There are four steps that I have identified to create a successful succession plan. The company must in its early years decide whether it is going to be sold or merged at the retirement of the founder, or continued under new management. You have to create a partnership agreement and organizational structure that provides for continuity. Also, you hire people who can do everything it takes to run a firm. At H&A, we hired and developed people with all the skills necessary to manage an accounting firm. In order to get good people, H&A told the people we hired that we were creating a firm that would not have to be sold when I retired. Another important element of the succession plan is to involve as many people as possible in the management of the firm. This includes the management committee, the partners-in-charge of the offices, the department heads, and those managing other important activities such as industry niche leaders. At H&A, we formed a management committee to be involved in the management of all the important aspects of the firm very early in our life. Also, we named Larry Unruh as the PIC of the Denver office in 2000. In this manner, key partners of the firm were able to work together for a long period of time in managing the firm. When the time for my retirement came, the partners knew each other well enough to make an informed decision as to future leadership. Finally, a detailed succession plan must be executed in the selection of the new managing partner.

I began implementing the succession plan for my retirement in May 2001. The goals of the succession plan were to pick the best person to be managing partner, to ensure that no one felt the process was unfair and left the firm, and to select a person who would be supported by all of the partners. In 2001, the two- to three-year detailed plan was created, a nominating committee was formed to make the final selections along with the management committee, and I was the bandleader.

The succession plan had many steps. Every partner evaluated every other partner in the firm on specific criteria. I interviewed every partner in the firm to ask about issues, concerns, and who they thought should be considered. Eventually, each partner evaluated candidates. They were rated by selection criteria. Everything during our process was confidential. I was the only one who saw all of the detail because I was the most independent person involved; my only interest was in having the process succeed.

Larry Unruh was selected by the nominating committee, and the ballots for the vote were sent out on June 4, 2002, my sixty-third birthday. Other partners were allowed to be on the ballot for the election of managing partner, if they so chose, with the support of the partners. Larry Unruh was elected managing partner and took office in January 2003. I served as Vice Chairman of the firm until my retirement on June 4, 2004.

Larry and Carole Unruh had some exciting times ahead of them. Larry naturally was concerned about following the founder as managing partner, but he obtained the support of the partners and all personnel of H&A to lead H&A in the future. That future, as is obvious today, was immensely successful.

The final important step to our successful succession plan was for me to get out of the way. Our home in Tonto Verde and a new motorcoach helped me let this happen.

Carole and Larry Unruh toast his election
to Managing Partner of H&A

Clarence practicing retirement in Barbados in 2003

Heinsight motorcoach

Clarence and Jane at Meat Cove, Cape North, Nova Scotia,
our northernmost point on our 2005 coach trip

Celebrating Clarence's retirement at the H&A partners' meeting
in Cabo San Lucas in 2004 – Todd, Michelle, Melanie, Mick,
Jane and Clarence

Don Horton, Lou Marinos, Clarence and Tom Easley
at Houston office party in 2005

Tonto Verde friends—Ted Petrowich, Charlotte Rousek, Gail
Petrowich and Mel Rousek—with Clarence at Lake Powell in 2008

H&A's Thirtieth Anniversary Party in Hawaii, 2007

Jane and Clarence celebrating their forty-fifth on
Canoun Island in the Grenadines

Jane and Clarence at Carp Lake in Montana

Heinsight leaving for the next destination

CHAPTER 14

OUR FAMILY

Jane and I are very happy in retirement and are unbelievably busy. Our two main hobbies are golf and travel. Our golf games are good enough to allow for many fun times with friends, our kids, and those we just hook up with during our travels or during club events. We have both seen enough airports so that our travels are mainly by motorcoach. We have traveled 35,000 miles in the coach in the last four years and expect to continue this activity for a few more years. We have been to the north coast of Prince Edward Island, which is as far as you can get from Phoenix without getting on a boat or airplane, and have also been to Vancouver Island and everywhere in between. In addition to golf and travel, we are active in community affairs, a little work related to board activities and the wrap-up of some old H&A projects, and mostly spending time with our family. I'm glad that I did not retire earlier than age sixty-five. In the big picture, work is very good for us, and we live so long that there's plenty of time to fool around and enjoy ourselves after retirement.

Our kids all got married later in life, which is the trend these days, so our grandkids are very young and range in age from six months to eight years.

Our oldest daughter, Melanie, was born in 1962. She received her B.S. degree in Mathematics in 1986 after completing college under the six-year plan. She received her Masters Degree in Education in 2001 in adult education and training with a minor in marketing. Melanie married Larry Fahrenbruch and they have one daughter, Madison, who is six.

In junior high school in Houston, Melanie helped her math teacher after school with daily lessons and preparing tests and grading them. The math teacher was an English teacher with no math education. In Houston teachers were bussed, rather than students, to comply with Federal integration rules. Obviously the quality of education suffered.

After graduating college in 1986, Melanie taught math at an alternative school near her home in Fort Collins. This turned into an emotional job, because some of the students attending the alternative school could not meet the terms of their probation and ended up going back to prison. Melanie then went into chamber of commerce work and became Vice President of the Fort Collins' Chamber of Commerce. She eventually decided to seek an opportunity in a smaller town as a president of a chamber of commerce and ended up in that position in Corvallis, Oregon. The Corvallis Chamber of Commerce received an award as the number-one chamber for towns its size in the United States. Melanie then went to work at Oregon State University in an executive position and had a very successful career in a university environment. One of her projects at OSU was to build the University's campus in Bend, Oregon, including obtaining the facilities and staffing the university. Melanie is now a director at the American Water Works Association, the largest organization of water engineers in the world.

In December 2006, Melanie and Larry asked me to talk to them about some terms for a job Larry was pursuing. After awhile, I asked Larry what he needed the other guy for. It was a good question, for within a week, Melanie and Larry had their new business distributing printing materials for businesses and government agencies cranked up. They are enjoying great success in just their second year of the company.

Our son Michael was born in 1970. He attended Colorado University and Colorado State University for a number of years studying college life. Eventually his sister, Melanie, convinced him to come to Oregon State University to complete his degree. Mick sold all of his assets and moved to Oregon. He graduated cum laude from OSU in 1999 with a Bachelors of Business Administration degree emphasizing information management. Mick surprised us all by being able to handle the math involved in getting a degree in information technology. Mick had attended kindergarten and started grade school in Houston, Texas. The Houston public schools were so bad that, when we moved back to Colorado, his teacher told him and us that he was too dumb to handle math and was never going to be a very good student. Fortunately, he had better teachers in grade school in Colorado; however, his math abilities were always a question mark to him until he handled calculus successfully at the college level.

Mick married Fanny Mimbela, a native of Peru, and they have two daughters. Michelle is two years old and Stephanie is six months old. Mick and Fanny were married at our house in Arizona and then had a formal wedding in Trujillo, Peru shortly thereafter. Going to Peru and being with Fanny's family is one of the highlights of all of our travels over many years. A bonus for attending the wedding in Peru was a side trip to Machu Picchu organized by Fanny.

Mick started his career with Intel Corp. in Portland, Oregon. Although he did well there and received major awards for system integration projects, that career ended when Intel shut down its mergers and acquisitions group. Mick is now with Countrywide Mortgage as Manager of the International Systems Solutions Group. The projects that he works on are over our heads so I cannot describe them here, but we do know they keep his attention 24/7. Mick has come a long way since his days in high school when he set the record for running out of gas in his car and calling his dad to help him out. Eventually, I kept an extra can of gas in the garage for the next call.

Michelle is our miracle daughter, born in 1975 in Houston, Texas. Michelle has a great self-image, which was recognized by everyone in the neighborhood early on. When Michelle was in the first grade, the kids were asked by the teacher to draw a picture of their family. On parent-teacher night, the pictures were posted around the classroom and drew many a laugh from people when they looked at Michelle's. In the middle of her picture was Michelle, much bigger than all of the other characters. The next-biggest figure on the picture was Genny, her Sheltie dog. The smallest images surrounding Michelle were her parents and siblings.

During her growing-up years in Genesee, Michelle was always involved with the swim team, which was amazingly successful for a mountain town with such cold weather. She continued on the swim team through high school and helped mentor the smaller kids. She was the only one that took the time to do this in the community. Michelle was trusted by the parents in Genesee and was even hired to baby-sit kids when their parents were out of town. My recollection is that she started working as a nanny on her own for some families when she was ten years old.

Michelle graduated from Fort Lewis in Durango, Colorado with a Bachelors Degree in Business Administration and a Minor in Accounting in 1998. Michelle guaranteed me when she left for college that she would be our first child to graduate in four years. However, her life took a few turns and it took her five years to get her degree. I didn't complain, since that was better than how long Melanie and Mick took. Michelle married Todd Wimett and they have two daughters, Ashlyn, who is two years old, and Zoe who is eight years old. Ashlyn is a lucky little girl. She looks likes her grandmother, Jane. Ashlyn started talking at eighteen months and at twenty months can carry on a pretty good conversation with her Grandpa.

Todd and Michelle own a own company that provides lighting for the entertainment industry in Los Angeles. Their projects include movies, television shows, commercials, and special events. Todd handles marketing and operations, and Michelle is a stay-at-home mom and handles the administrative side of the business.

After graduating from college, Michelle worked as an internal auditor for an insurance company, a bank, and eventually for California Institute of Technology. Before her CalTech job, Michelle was a member of the audit staff of Arthur Andersen in Denver. She did well in this career, and as a second-year staff she taught a training class to the partners and managers in the use of electronic auditing.

We are a very fortunate family in that all of our kids are in constant communication with each other. They talk to each other frequently, and we all socialize and have a lot of fun together. We are also fortunate that our grandkids like Grandma and Grandpa. Whenever Mick and Fanny discipline Michelle, she goes to her room and gets her suitcase and stands by the front door demanding to go to Grandpa's house. Our other grandkids are the same. They often cry when they have to leave Grandpa's house to go home.

Our son Mitch was born in 1960 and disappeared in the spring of 1982 at the age of twenty-two. This has been very difficult for our family, and the sadness of losing Mitch is not something that we will ever get over. All of the stories that you read in newspapers about the trauma of having a missing child are true. Many times, leads for the location of a missing person come up; however, they are almost all generally unsuccessful. The ups and downs are hard to deal with, but I think we all now realize that he probably will never be found.

Mitch was a gifted child. When he was five, his kindergarten teacher came to our house to tell us that he was the most intelligent child she had ever taught during her thirty-year career. Mitch never took advantage of his intelligence, but rather became enamored with football. He worked hard on weights and training and eventually became fast enough to make all conference his senior year and get quite a bit of interest from colleges. Mitch did a number of things that amazed us. Two of them involved overhauling car engines that he had no training in or experience with. The family of his girlfriend in Houston had an Oldsmobile car that didn't run well. Mitch was sixteen when he took the V-8 engine apart, overhauled it, and put it back together so that the kids could take it to college. Another time, after we had moved back to Colorado, one of our neighbors had the engine of a Mustang torn up and lying on their garage floor. The father who had taken it apart had personal problems and never got around to putting it back together. Mitch went over to their house, put the engine back together, and got the car running. I still wonder how a kid could have those kinds of skills. After a year of college, Mitch decided to see the world. He sailed freighters in the Caribbean, worked in the oil fields, and lived on a sailboat that he rebuilt in Houston, Texas. The sailboat was owned by Racehorse Haynes, one of the most famous criminal lawyers in the United States. Mitch was last home for Christmas in 1981. He told us that he would always come home for Christmas, no matter what he was doing. He has not returned for Christmas, but we are still hopeful.

There are two stories involving Jane's family that also need to be told. They involve Jane's family farm in Sidney and the ranch in western Montana.

In the late 60s, Jane's dad, Al, was running short of cash and had missed some payments on his loan with the Sidney farm as collateral. The bank threatened to foreclose, which irritated Al very much. He ignored the bank, and they went through a foreclosure process and sold the farm to a lady married to my uncle. In Montana, there is a one-year grace period during which a foreclosed property can be redeemed. One day before the court date to finalize the sale to my aunt, Al went to Sidney, Montana and waited patiently at the Cheerio Bar for a small plane to arrive in Sidney carrying $100,000 in twenty-dollar bills in a suitcase. At nine o'clock that night, Al went to the small Sidney airport and received the suitcase. The next day at the court hearing, the judge told Al that he was very sorry but that he was going to have to transfer title of the farm to my aunt. Al stood up and told the judge that he was going to pay off the loan, and dumped $100,000 in twenty dollar bills on the courtroom table. He told the judge that he wanted his title back. The judge told my aunt that he was sorry but that the title was going to be retained by Al. My aunt became quite upset because she had a large investment in planting crops on the farm that would, under Montana law, stay with the property. She screamed to the judge, "He gets the farm and the crops. What do I get?" Al turned to my aunt and said, "You get f——!"

Our ranch in western Montana had a lien on it, and eventually Al and the bank agreed that if the loan was not paid off by a specific date, the bank would take title of the ranch in 1997. If the loan was paid off, Al would get the title back. The loans on the ranch were all related to the oil boom of the 80s. During the oil boom, Al was involved in real estate development and other activities supported by the oil industry. When the oil bust occurred, property values declined and cash to pay off debts dried up.

I had a very strong personal commitment to never get involved in family business. However, it was difficult for me to handle the fact that the bank was going to get the ranch for payment of a $350,000 loan when the ranch was worth in the range of $1 million. I finally told Jane's parents that if they would put the ranch in a trust totally controlled by me, I would buy the ranch under the trust. Under the terms of the trust, all the proceeds of the ranch would be given to Jane's parents after paying all of the loans and costs I would incur in holding and selling the ranch. They agreed to my terms, and the Colorado National Bank was very instrumental in getting all of the appraisals and paperwork done in order to make a loan to the trust for me to execute the transaction. One day before the meeting in Butte, Montana to transfer the title, I got a cashier's check from Colorado National Bank for $350,000, and got on an airplane and flew to Butte, Montana. The next morning, at the meeting with representatives of the bank and Jane's parents, I handed the bank the check to pay off the loan and picked up the title to the ranch.

These two stories are related because if I had not known about the first story about helping someone in trouble, I may not have been willing to help with the ranch. The cash to pay off the loan for the Sidney farm came from an old business associate to whom Al had given money to rescue him from foreclosure in some motels that he had built. When asked, the associate put the $100,000 in cash on the plane and sent it to Sidney to bail Al out. The western Montana ranch could not be sold because everybody knew about the terms of the deal with the bank. Therefore, everybody waited for the bank to foreclose to try to get a bargain purchase of the ranch. After it was put into the trust controlled by me, sales activity picked up and the ranch was sold within a year for $1 million.- I was very happy to give the proceeds to Jane's parents who enjoyed that cash to the fullest during their lifetimes.

Melanie, Larry and Madison

Todd, Michelle, Ashlyn and Zoe

Mick, Michelle, Stephanie and Fanny

Melanie shows dad her engagement ring at Christmas, 1995

Family picture in our Genesee backyard in 1995

Clarence and Mick on their annual golf and fishing trip in Calgary

Jane and Clarence at Machu Pichu, Peru, 2005

Clarence and Jane in the Andes of Peru, 2005